I0462782

YOUR
UNICORN
BUSINESS

by Julie Rowland

COPYRIGHT AND DISCLAIMER

This material is copyright. No part, in whole or in part, may be reproduced by any process, or any other exclusive right exercised, without the permission of QuadriviumBusinessAcademy.com © 2019

Julie Rowland

Published by:
Leader Publishing Worldwide
19 Axford Bay
Port Moody, BC V3H 3R4
Tel: 1 888 294 9151
Fax: 1 877 575 9151

DISCLAIMER AND/OR LEGAL NOTICES:
While every attempt has been made to verify information provided in this book, neither the author nor the publisher assumes any responsibility for any errors, omissions or inaccuracies.

Any slights of people or organizations are unintentional. If advice concerning legal or related matters is needed, the services of a qualified professional should be sought. This book is not intended as a source of legal or accounting advice. You should be aware of any laws which govern business transactions or other business practices in your state or province.

The income statements and examples are not intended to represent or guarantee that everyone will achieve the same results. Everyone's success will be determined by his or her desire, dedication, effort, and motivation. There are no guarantees you will duplicate the results stated here, because you recognize that any business endeavor has inherent risk for loss of capital.

Any reference to any persons or business, whether living or deceased, is purely coincidental.

DEDICATION

For my children, Emily and Christopher. You are strong, beautiful, and the best things in my life. You can make me smile and cry and that is how I know how deeply you are loved. I am so proud to say I am your mother.

Devon and Eliza are wonderful partners for you and now we have Zachary (the boy), Lexi (the dog) and Ronnie (the cat) to round out the family. And hopefully, more grandchildren to come….. a grandmother's selfish wish!

I am blessed with the best family!

I love you all,
Mom

DEDICATION

CONTENTS

CONTENTS

INTRODUCTION

"Progress always involves risks. You can't steal second base and keep your foot on first."

Robert Quillen (1887-1948), journalist and humorist

I love that quote because it is as true today as it was in the late 1880's. It is a great reminder that risk is a necessary part of life if you want to achieve anything great. By opening this book, you've taken that first step. Congratulations in your quest to enhance your business and marketing skills.

Even though I truly believe we are all two great marketing ideas away from more sales opportunities than we can fully imagine, it takes much more than marketing to reach that next level. The strategies in this book, when implemented with precision and care, are guaranteed to make you more money with less effort. These are strategies that have helped businesses just like yours make hundreds of thousands of dollars, including your competitors.

According to Bloomberg, eight out of ten entrepreneurs who start businesses fail within the first 18 months. A whopping 80% crash and burn. I have dedicated myself to helping business owners, because I know many of the companies that failed, could have succeeded with some direction. Entrepreneurs start their business because they have a talent, a skill, or a product to sell. They do not know how to run a business. They opened their business, hung out their shingle, but never set the proper foundation to hold that business up and allow it to be as successful as they dreamed.

As you read the book remember it does not matter what industry you are in or what type of business you operate (I've been part of many). What matters is that you grasp the heart of the principles and the underlying lessons and strategies, that can help grow any operation in any category of business imaginable.

The best time to start is NOW, not tomorrow, not next week or next year. Leave your competitors behind and steal second base!

To your success,

Julie Rowland

1

Use Goal Setting Effectively

We've all heard about the power of setting goals. Everyone has seen statistics that connect goal setting to success in both your business life and your personal life. I'm sure if I asked you today what your goals are, you could rattle off a few wants and hopes without thinking too long.

However, what most people do not realize is that the power of goal setting lies in *writing goals down*. Committing goals to paper and reviewing them regularly gives you a 95% higher chance of achieving your desired outcomes. Studies have shown that only three to five percent of people in the world have written goals. The same three to five percent who achieve success in business and earn considerable wealth.

These studies have also found that by retirement, only four percent of people in the world will have enough accumulated wealth to maintain their income level and quality of life. As a business owner, it is essential that you develop a plan for your retirement, but it is equally essential that you develop a plan for your success.

This chapter focuses on the power of goal setting as part of your business success. I'll teach you to set SMART goals that are rooted in your own personal value system and supporting techniques to achieve your goals faster.

What are Goals?

Goals are clear targets that are attached to a specific time frame and action plan. They focus your efforts and drive your motivation in a clear direction. Goals are different from dreams in that goals outline a plan of action, while dreams are a conceptual vision of your wish or desired outcome.

Goals require work; work on yourself, work for your business, and work for others. You cannot achieve a goal, no matter how badly you want it, without being prepared to make a considerable effort. If you are ready to invest your time and energy, goals will help you:

- Realize a dream or wish for your personal or business life
- Make a change in your life; add positivity or remove negativity
- Improve your skills and performance ability
- Start or change a habit, positive or negative

Why Set Goals?

As we've already reviewed, setting goals and committing them to paper is the most effective way to cultivate success. The most important reason to set a goal is **to attach a clear action plan to a desired outcome.**

Goals help focus our time and energy on one (or several) key outcomes at a time. Many business owners have hundreds of ideas whirling around in their heads at any one time, on top of daily responsibilities. By writing down and focusing on a few ideas at a time, you can prioritize and concentrate your efforts, avoid being stretched too thin, and produce greater results.

Since goals attach action to outcomes, goals can help to break down big dreams into manageable (and achievable) sections. Creating a multi-goal strategy will put a road map in place to help you get to your desired outcome. If your goal is to start a pizza business and make six figures a year, there are a number of smaller steps to complete before you achieve your end result.

Success doesn't happen by itself. It is the result of consistent and committed action by an individual who is driven to achieve something. Success means something different for everyone, so creating goals is a personal endeavor. Goals can be large and small, personal and public, financial and spiritual. It is not the size of the goal that matters; what matters is that you write the goal down and commit to making the effort required to achieve it.

What happens when I achieve a goal?

You should congratulate yourself and your team, of course! By rewarding yourself and your team after every achievement, you not only train your mind to associate hard work with reward but develop loyalty among your employees.

You should also ask yourself if your achievement can be taken to the next level, or if your goal can be stretched by building on the effort you have already made. Consistently setting new and higher targets will lay the framework for constant improvement and personal and professional growth.

Power of Positive Thinking

When was the last time you tuned into your internal stream of consciousness? What does the stream of thoughts that run through your mind sound like? Are they positive? Negative? Are they logical? Reasonable?

Positive thinking and healthy self-talk are the most important business tools you can ever cultivate. By programming a positive stream of subconscious thoughts into your mind, you can control your reality, and ultimately your success. Think about someone you know who is constantly negative; someone who complains and whines and makes excuses for their unhappiness. How successful are they? How do their fears and doubts become reality in their world?

You are what you continuously believe about yourself and your environment. If you focus your mind on something in your mental world, it will nearly always manifest as reality in your physical world.

Positive thinking is a key part of setting goals. You won't achieve your goal until you believe that you can. You will achieve your goals faster when you believe in yourself, and the people around you who are helping to make your goal a reality.

Successful people are rooted in a strong belief system. Belief in themselves, belief in the work they are doing, and belief in the people around them. They are motivated to improve and learn, but also confident in their existing skills and knowledge. Their positive attitude and energy is clearly felt in everything they do.

Ever notice how complainers usually surround themselves with other complainers? The same is true of positive thinkers. If you cultivate an upbeat and positive attitude, you will be surrounded by people who share your values and outlook on life. Too often, people and our society subscribe to a continuous stream of negative chatter. The more you hear it, the more you'll believe it.

How many times have you heard someone say the following?

- That's impossible.
- Don't even bother.
- It's already been done.
- We tried that, and it didn't work.

- You're too young.

- You're too old.

- You'll never get there.

- You'll never get that done.

Positive thinking and positive influences will provide the support you need to achieve your goals. Choose your friends and close colleagues wisely
and surround yourself with positive thinkers. Be the person that successful people want to be with.

Creating SMART Goals

SMART goals are just that: smart. Whether you are setting goals for your personal life, your business, or with your employees, goals that have been developed with the SMART principle have a higher probability of being achieved.

The SMART Principle

1. Specific

Specific goals are clearer and easier to achieve than nonspecific goals. When writing down your goal, ask yourself the five "W" questions to narrow in on what exactly you are aiming for. Who? Where? What? When? Why?

For example, instead of a nonspecific goal like, "get in shape for the summer," a specific goal would be, "go to the gym three times a week and eat twice as many vegetables."

2. Measurable

If you can't measure your goal, how will you know when you've achieved it? Measurable goals help you clearly see where you are, and where you want to be. You can see change happen as it happens.

Measurable goals can also be broken down and managed in smaller pieces. They make it easier to create an action plan or identify the steps required to achieve your goal. You can track your progress, revise your plan, and celebrate each small achievement. For example, instead of aiming to increase revenue in 2019, you can set out to increase revenue by 30% in the next 12 months and celebrate each 10% along the way.

3. Achievable

Goals that are achievable have a higher chance of being realized. While it is important to think big, and dream big, too often people set goals that are simply beyond their capabilities and wind up disappointed. Goals can stretch you, but they should always be feasible to maintain your motivation and commitment.

If you want to complete your first triathlon but you've never run a mile in your life, you would be setting a goal that was beyond your current capabilities. If you decided instead to train for a five-mile race in six months, you would be setting an achievable goal.

4. Relevant

Relevant or realistic goals are goals that have a logical place in your life or your overall business strategy. The goal's action plan can be reasonably integrated into your life, with a realistic amount of effort.

If your goal is to train to climb to base camp at Mount Everest within one year and you're about to launch a start-up business, you may need to question the relevance of your goal in the context of your current commitments.

5. Timely

It is essential for every goal to be attached to a timeframe, otherwise it is merely a dream. Check in to make sure that your timeframe is realistic; not too short, or too long. This will keep you motivated and committed to your action plan, and allow you track your progress.

Autosuggestion + Visualization

Autosuggestion and visualization are two techniques that can assist you in achieving your goals. Some of the most well-known and successful people in the world use these techniques, and it is not coincidence that they are masters in their own fields of business and sport. A few of these people include:

- Michael Phelps (Olympic Swimmer)
- Andre Agassi (Tennis)
- Wayne Gretzky (Hockey)
- Bill Gates (Microsoft)
- Walt Disney (Entertainment)

Of course, each of these people have a high degree of talent, ambition, intelligence and drive. However, to reach the top of their respective field, they have each used Autosuggestion and Visualization.

Autosuggestion

Autosuggestion is your internal dialogue; the constant stream of thoughts and comments that flows through your mind and impacts what you think about yourself and how you perceive situations.

Since you were a small child, this self-talk has been influenced by your experiences and has programmed your mind to think and react in certain ways. The good news is that you can reprogram your mind and customize your self-talk any way you like. That is the power of Autosuggestion.

To begin practicing Autosuggestion, make sure you are relaxed and open to trying the technique. An ideal time is just before bed, or when you have some time to sit quietly. Then, repeat positive affirmations to yourself about the ideal outcome. Top sports and businesspeople will often practice just before a big game or meeting.

Some examples of positive self-talk or autosuggestion include:

- I will lead my team to a victory tonight!
- I will be relaxed open to meeting new people at the party tonight!
- I will deliver a clear and impacting speech!
- I will stop worrying and tackle this problem tomorrow!
- I will stand up for my own ideas in the meeting!
- I will remember everything I have studied for the test tomorrow!

Visualization

Visualization is a practice complementary to Autosuggestion. While you can repeat affirmations to yourself over and over, combining this practice with visualization is twice as powerful.

Visualization is exactly what it sounds like; repeatedly visualizing how something is going to happen in your mind's eye. Nearly everyone in sports practices this technique. It has been proven to enhance performance better than practice alone.

This technique can easily be applied to business. It is appropriate prior to any presentation or meeting where you must speak, present or "perform." You can also visualize yourself being incredibly productive and effective in your office. It can even work so you have a discussion with your spouse calmly and rationally.

Elements to think about during visualization:

- What does the room look like?
- What do the people in the room look like?
- What is their mood? How do they receive me?
- What image do I project?
- How do I look?
- How do I behave? What is my attitude?
- What is the outcome?

2

How to Profit through Time Management

Manage Time Like Money

Why did you get into business for yourself? Was it to be your own boss? Choose your own hours? Have more time with the family? Spend more time doing what you love? Chances are, you answered yes to all these questions.

These days, you probably wonder where the time went. Why you spent 12 hours at work and barely make a dent in your to-do list. We already know that time is a key resource for you and your business, but it's also a key resource in your life. Harnessing and leveraging time is the only way to enjoy life and have a profitable business at the same time.

Most business owners carefully manage their financial and personnel resources and pay due attention to their performance. Marketing plans and budgets are created. People are hired and fired. What most business owners don't realize is that time, and the time of all employees, requires the same attention and diligent management.

Time will never manage itself. The decision to make a pro-active effort to manage your time must come from you. Once you have committed to taking ownership for your own time management, there are a host of tools available to you. But first, you must understand how much your time is actually worth, and where you are currently spending it.

14

What is Your Time Worth?

Ever wonder what your time is actually worth? Here's a quick way to figure it out:

Target annual income	A.
Working days in a year	B. 235
Working hours in a day	C. 7
Working hours in a year	D. 1,645
A ÷ D = YOUR HOURLY WORTH (before tax + expenses)	E.

This is a very simple calculation intended to put your time in perspective. In reality, no one is productive for each of the 1,645 hours. Various studies have put actual productivity at anywhere between 25 minutes and four hours per day. Either way, there's a lot of room for improvement.

Let's look at it another way:

Your age	A.
Days in a year	B.
Days spent on earth to date (A x B)	C.
Average life expectancy	D. 75
Total projected days on earth (D x B)	E.
Estimated days left (E – C)	F.

This exercise isn't intended to scare you but bring your attention to the importance of choosing how you spend each hour you have available. It is a choice! By developing the skills required to manage your time, you will not only have a profitable business, but a rewarding and balanced life.

The Five Culprits of Time Theft

Chances are, if you're like most people, you have no idea where your time goes. You're likely frustrated by the fact that you can spend 10, 12, even 14 hours a day working, and be in the same place you began the day. Or you were only able to bill for half of those hours.

When we're too busy and overloaded with work, we often switch into reactive mode. We can't make it to the bottom of the pile so end up handling issues and making decisions at the last minute. One of the great benefits of choosing to become proactive in time management is that you can become proactive in all other areas of your business. When in proactive mode, you can take steps to grow your business through networking, building programs, and establishing systems.

Before you investigate where your time goes, let's look at the top five culprits of modern-day time theft:

1. Your Email

How many times a day do you check your email? Is Outlook or Mail constantly running on your desktop? Email – internal, external, personal and business – clogs up your day like no other communication channel. For many of us, it is possible to spend the entire day writing and responding to emails without even glancing at our inbox. The number of emails sent and received each day by the average person in 2017 was 147. Multiply that by an average of two minutes per message, and you have spent almost five hours on email in a single day.

2. Your Cell Phone

Cell phones have created convenience, security, and the luxury of telecommuting, but they didn't originally call them a Blackberry for nothing. PDAs and cell phones have also created a society that expects to be able to reach you at any moment, or at least receive instant responses to their calls. You cell phone or PDA not only robs you of your time during the day, but also during the evenings and on weekends when you are not at work.

3. Your Open-Door Policy

If you make it easy for your staff and associates to interrupt you, they will. Too often, open-door policies are set up by human resource departments to create clear communication channels. Instead, they create a clog of employees lined up at your door seeking immediate answers to non-emergency issues.

4. Meetings

How many times have you been to a meeting that was scheduled to be an hour, and ended up lasting three? How often do you attend unnecessary meetings? Or meetings that run off-topic? Meetings can be a huge source of wasted time. Your valuable time. In a senior management or ownership position, your day may consist of back-to-back meetings, leaving only your evening hours to complete the tasks that should have been done during the day.

5. YOU!

Every person has daily habits that sabotage their ability to work productively and efficiently. Many entrepreneurs and business owners can't separate business hours from leisure hours. Some get caught in a time warp while surfing the internet. Others, mainly overachievers, can become paralyzed by perfectionism or procrastination. Mainly we just don't have the tools to schedule and structure our time in a way that fits with our working style.

Where Does Your Time Go?

So far, we've seen that time is a resource that should be as carefully managed as cash. We have figured out what your time is worth and looked at the top five culprits of time theft. You've committed to taking steps to become a better time manager. What now?

Personal Time Management Research Exercise

The next step is to take a good, (and honest!) look at how you spend your time. Once you understand your patterns and habits, you begin to implement the strategies in this chapter that will make you a better time manager.

Step One: Time Audit

Use the Time Log Worksheet at the back of this chapter to record how you spend your time for three working days in a row. Be honest and be specific. Include time spent in transit, surfing the web, interacting with clients and colleagues, as well as how your time is spent at home in the evenings. The more information you can record, the easier it will be to analyze your time management skills in step two.

Step Two: Time Categorization

Once you have recorded your time for three days, sit down with all three sheets in front of you and identify the following, using different colored markers or highlighters:

- Driving, public transportation or other travel

- Eating, including food preparation
- Personal Errands
- Exercise
- Watching TV
- Sleeping, including naps
- Using the computer, personal use only
- Being with family / friends
- Emailing, including checking, reading, and returning messages
- Talking on the phone, including checking and returning messages
- Internal meetings
- External meetings
- Administrative work
- Client work
- Non-client, non-administrative work

Step Three: Time Analysis

Now that you have identified how you have spent your time, go through the worksheets one more time and identify if you have spent enough, too much, or too little time on each main task.

Then, based on your observations, answer the following questions:

1. What patterns do you notice about how you spend your time during the day? (i.e., When are you most productive? Least productive? Most or least interrupted?)

_____

_____

_____

_____

_____

2. Write down the four highest priorities in your life right now. Does your timesheet reflect these priorities?

_____

_____

_____

_____

3. If you have more time, what would you do?

_____

_____

_____

_____

4. If you had less time, what wouldn't you do?

_____

_____

_____

_____

5. Could you remove the items in question four and add the items in question three? Why or why not?

_____

_____

_____

_____

_____

6. Is procrastination a problem for you? How much?

_____

_____

_____

_____

_____

Strategies for Profitable Time Management

There are many ways to curb time theft and refine your time management ability. Through a solid understanding of how you currently spend and waste time, you can determine which strategies you need to implement to correct unproductive behavior.

Here are 17 ways you can turn **less** of your time into **more** money:

1. Set Clear Priorities

The foundation of time management is having a clear understanding of what your time is best spent on. Once you accept that you can't do everything, you need to decide what needs to be completed now, what can be completed later, and what someone else can complete. Each to-do list you create should be put through this filter and reorganized so the highest priority items are on top, and the lowest priority items are less visible, or on the bottom.

Once you have established your priorities, which will also naturally reflect the priorities and goals of your business, stick to them. Just because someone else feels something is of a high priority doesn't mean it holds the same status next to your other tasks.

Prioritization is also helpful in your personal life and leisure time. Your spare time is precious! Make sure are clear on how you would like to spend it.

2. Use Your Skills – Delegate Your Weaknesses

As a business owner, your day naturally consists of tasks you dislike doing. Some are essential; signing checks, reviewing financial statements, and other business maintenance, while others are simply not within your skill set.

If you are a strong public speaker, but struggle with report writing, delegate to a copywriter or editor. If you own a retail store and have no experience in design, outsource your signage. These freelance professionals often cost half as much as you and take half as long to complete the task. Your time is saved for tasks that use and strengthen your skills effectively, your stress is managed, and ultimately a better product is produced.

3. Delegate, Delegate, Delegate

As a small business owner, the only way you will ever get everything done is by delegating. Delegation is a vital skill that needs to be refined and practiced, and once mastered is the key to profitable time management.

Too often, owners and managers believe that it will be "faster" or "more efficient" to complete the task themselves than to train and monitor someone else. Other times, there are no internal resources to download assignments to.

As a result, the following trends can be seen in many small companies:

- Owners and senior staff are stressed and overworked, while junior staff are underutilized and under capacity.
- Staff members are not given an opportunity to grow and develop in their roles and may perceive a lack of trust or confidence in their ability. The company may lose good people.
- Owners and senior staff are always in a reactive state, instead of a visionary or proactive state.
- Delegation happens at the very last minute, and junior staff has little understanding of either the overall project or expectations for the task.

The easiest way to fix this problem is before it starts. Create a solid team of staff members around you who are well-trained and prepared to support the business. Attract and retain qualified and quality people who can be cross-trained and promoted within the company. Ensure that communication flows throughout the business, so everyone has the product and service knowledge to step in and assist when necessary.

4. Learn to Say "No"

It's easy to fall into the habit of saying yes to everything. You are, after all the business owner. No one can complete these tasks as well as you. You'll lose that customer if you don't help them with their garage sale, right?

Wrong!! The most successful business owners have a keen understanding of how their time is best spent, and *delegate* the remaining responsibilities to trusted others. It's too easy to say yes to every request in the moment, and later feel overwhelmed when it's added to your to do list. You may not ruffle any feathers, but what toll does it take on your stress level? Your workload? Your time is valuable, so protect it!

Remember that if it is too challenging to say no immediately, you can always request some time to think about it. This way, you can evaluate your workload and realistically decide whether you can take on a new project. Then, stand by your decision, or assist in bringing in the necessary resources to get it done.

5. Create (and keep!) a Strict Schedule

While multi-tasking is a desirable skill, it is also often a time thief. Attempting to do too many things at one time ensures that nothing gets done. As a business owner, you need to be able to focus and concentrate on essential projects without interruptions.

The only way to do this is the commit to a strict schedule. Once you understand your work style and concentration patterns, you can allocate periods of the day to specific tasks. This includes both personal and leisure time. Schedule it and stick to it.

Schedule time for: list-creation and prioritization, email messages, telephone messages, internal meetings, client meetings, meeting preparation, "me-time", family time, recreation and fitness, daily business tasks, and blocks for focused work. Remember that there is a training period involved in beginning a new routine for yourself and those around you. Use your voicemail, out-of-office email message, and a closed door to begin to let people know when you will not be disturbed.

6. Make Decisions

The choice not to make a decision, is a decision in itself. The most successful business owners make good decisions quickly and efficiently, and do not waste time deliberating over simple choices.

In leadership positions, often people are afraid of making the wrong decision or looking foolish if they make a mistake in front of junior staff. What they don't realize, is that hesitating or avoiding decision making impacts their leadership just as much or more than making the wrong decision. Not only can being indecisive be personally stressful, but it is also stressful for those around you whose tasks are waiting on your choices.

You must make the best decision with the information you have, in the time frame you have, to make the decision. No one expects you to be a fortune teller. Be decisive, make some mistakes and learn from them.

7. Manage Telephone Interruptions

This is a huge source of time theft that can easily be managed and avoided. If you are available to take phone calls at any time of day, you are setting yourself up to take work home in the evenings. The phone will always ring when you are focused on an important task, and this is something can easily be avoided.

Figure out when you are most productive. Is it in the morning or the afternoon? Before, during, or after lunch? Once you have identified this time period, set your phone on "do not disturb" or have your calls directed to voicemail. If you do not have a receptionist, a variety of automatic answering systems are available for a nominal fee. To structure your phone time further, let callers know on your voicemail what specific time of day is best to reach you via phone. Then, set that time aside to receive and return phone calls.

8. Keep Your Work Environment Organized

Have you ever tried to make dinner in a messy kitchen? More of your time is spent looking for (and cleaning) dishes and tools then actually spent cooking the meal.

The same goes for your work environment. If your desk and office are in a constant state of chaos, then you mind will be too. In fact, some studies have revealed that the average senior business leader spends nearly four weeks each year navigating through messy or cluttered desks, looking for lost information. Does that sound like productive time to you?

Once you make the initial clean sweep, it's easy to maintain order in the chaos:

- Tidy your desk at the beginning and end of each day. Attach pertinent documents to your to do list or have clear and organized folders for loose papers.
- Organize your supplies drawer so you have easy access to stationery like pens, post-it notes, staplers and highlighters. Every minute counts!
- Only have the documents and files you are working on, on your desk. The rest should be neatly filed on a side table for later retrieval.
- Keep personal items (like photos or memorabilia) out of your primary line of vision. These can be distracting and encourage daydreaming.

As for your office or store, there are many ways to make its layout more conducive to effective time management. Try:

- Minimizing the distance between the reception desk and electronics like photocopies and fax machines.
- Keep a clear line of sight between your office and the most productive area of your business, so you are aware of what is happening amongst your staff.
- Organize shelves and filling cabinets so files are not only easily accessed, but out of sight when not being used. Consider putting sliding doors or cabinets in storage areas and remember that the floor is not a storage cabinet.

9. Keep Your Filing System Organized

If your data isn't organized properly, you will waste hundreds of hours searching for documents you need on a regular basis. This includes both electronic and hard copy files; they need to be organized and up to date.

Customer databases and inquiry records are worth their weight in gold. You can't afford to get behind when updating this information, or poorly store it for later retrieval. There are many easy to use software programs that will manage and organize customer databases for you; it doesn't need to be a time consuming or tedious exercise.

A simple way to manage information is to keep it in short, medium, and long-term files for both hard and electronic copies. Create shortcuts on your desktop for folders or files you constantly access. Have short-term files available on your desk, medium-term files available within an arm's reach, and long-term files stored in cabinets.

10. Clearly Communicate – Never Assume

One of the biggest issues for time management in business is miscommunication. This is a dangerous issue that can cripple any business, including yours. Establishing and enforcing clear policies on things like accurate note taking, task assignments, and phone messages will ensure your staff understand the importance of clear and accurate communication.

The easiest habit to start to curb miscommunication is simple: write everything down. Carry a notepad, and jot down key points, figures, agreements and deadlines. Don't assume you'll remember later. You have at least a hundred other things to remember.

Some other simple strategies are:

- Return all communication promptly, including email, letters, faxes and phone calls
- Repeat back phone messages, phone numbers and other figures to confirm you recorded the information correctly.
- Record appointments in your PDA or agenda the moment you make them. Otherwise, you will forget.
- Double check and confirm everything – addresses, phone numbers, meeting locations and times.
- Maintain accurate customer contact logs with dates, times, and phone numbers.
- Post checklists in your store or office for routine operations procedures.
- Announce any changes to the policies and procedures manual immediately.

11. Stop Duplicating Efforts

This is a key element of time management that is closely related to effective communication. Studies have continually shown that many businesses often duplicate and triplicate efforts that need to be completed once.

When you have clear systems and procedures in place, your staff will not need to "reinvent the wheel" each time the task needs to be completed. Meeting minutes and individual task assignments will ensure everyone is on the same page and understands their personal responsibilities.

Simple examples of this include re-reading your to-do list each hour to determine what the next important item is. If your list is already structured by priority, this is a needless task. If two staff members are working on similar projects, but unaware of the other, the work will not only be inconsistent, but the efforts will be duplicated. These are easy problems to fix, once they have been identified and communicated.

12. Say Goodbye to Procrastination and Perfectionism

Procrastination is something we all face at one time or another and likely have since our school days. However, given the pace that the world operates at today, you will only fall behind your competitor if you allow procrastination to rule your day. So how you do avoid it? If you are an instant gratification person, place a couple of the easiest tasks at the beginning of your
list. This will give you the necessary boost to keep going. If you constantly put off the hardest task until the end of the day, hoping you do not get to it, DO IT FIRST! Reward yourself by crossing each step off your to-do list.

Many small business owners also fall victim to perfectionism, which can be paralyzing. The fear that there isn't enough time or resources to "get it perfect" will sometimes stop you dead in your tracks. Perfectionism can also hinder your ability to delegate tasks you believe no one else can complete "better". Do the best you can with the time and resources you have and just get started.

13. Plan Your Work, Work Your Plan

Have you ever placed an advertisement on the fly because it was "cheaper", "faster", or "more urgent" than creating a marketing plan? Do you and your staff have a clear idea of where your business is headed over the next six to 12 months, or five years?

Many studies show that less than 10% of small businesses have up to date marketing and business plans, as compared to most large corporations and publicly traded companies, which have both.

Marketing and business plans take time and effort to create. But they work and pay off many times over. They also save you time and money as compared to a haphazard or fly-by-the-seat-of-your-pants strategy. With a marketing plan in place, you will have an idea of how many ads you will be placing in a year, which will earn you a volume discount. Your marketing materials will complement each other and deliver the same message to the same target audience. Designers will charge less for a package of materials than for individual items.

You must first set your marketing budget so that you can allocate monies over a period of time and not run out mid-way through the year. Spending on future income for year-end marketing may leave your pockets empty when marketing is need most.

A business plan will provide you with a guide to reference when making decisions. You can repeatedly ask if the endeavor at hand will contribute to your overall vision, or just seems like a good idea or price. Every business decision you make must get you closer to realizing your vision or it is an incorrect or unnecessary decision.

Remember that planning includes both short and long-term time frames, and applies to both your daily to-do list, and your marketing budget.

It provides you with a means to measure your progress, assists in identifying priorities, and helps to manage your time.

14. Avoid Needless, Impromptu and Unstructured Meetings

This may seem like a time theft issue that is out of your control, but it's not. You are in control of your own time, and through strict scheduling you can establish a structure for internal and external meetings that everyone around you can work within.

Minimize impromptu internal meetings by letting your staff know when you're available for a "quick chat" and when you are not. If it is important, ask them to schedule a time to meet with you that works with both of your schedules. This not only saves you time but encourages staff to find solutions to their own issues, and only approach you with more urgent or challenging matters.

You can't avoid having meetings, but you can avoid having unstructured meetings. Ask for or create an agenda for each meeting you attend, with a clear objective and an amount of time allocated to each item. This will keep your meetings focused and on task. If a meeting does run late, give yourself a reasonable buffer, and politely leave for your next appointment. You can always follow up with a colleague to catch-up on the pertinent items you may have missed.

15. Establish Clear Policies and Procedures

A clear policy and procedure manual is like a marketing or business plan. It takes time to create, but ultimately saves everyone in your company time, money and effort. A step-by-step guide to "the way we do things here" is an invaluable resource for your existing and new staff, and provides clear expectations for how you like things done.

Too many businesses make up policies and procedures quickly to solve an individual problem. This creating dangerous scenarios where mistakes are made, and expectations are not clear. Some items that should be included in a comprehensive policy and procedures manual include:

- Recruitment
- Customer relations
- Customer inquiries
- Customer complaints
- Returns
- Exchanges
- Late Payments
- Job Descriptions

- Business hours
- Salary structure
- Bonus structure
- Employee review
- Theft
- Harassment

16. Keep the Right Set of Tools

The equipment your business needs to operate and grow effectively should always be on hand, or easily contracted out. This is specific to each company, and closely related to costs, including the cost of your time.

Whether you are a high-tech business or local retailer, knowledge of the latest advancements in technology will increase your efficiency. It will help you stay on top of the competitor, maintain your position as an expert, and perhaps provide an easier way of getting things done. Always ask yourself if these purchases are essential to your business. Could perhaps making these purchases from a second-hand dealer minimize cost? Is it more cost effective to outsource or sub-contract the tasks to someone with access to this equipment, instead of buying the equipment yourself?

If your business relies on tools and technology for daily tasks (such as the trades profession) then obtaining the best quality machinery you can afford is crucial.

17. Maintain Your Equipment

This may seem obvious, but you'll understand the importance if your network server has ever crashed or point of sale system has malfunctioned. Your business can be slowed to a stand-still if your equipment is not in good working order. Of course, there are instances that can't be predicted, but regular maintenance of your essential equipment will reduce these occurrences and help to anticipate when old equipment needs to be repaired or replaced. Having the same staff member perform the maintenance each month will also minimize cost.

Personal Time Management Strategy

Choose the top four tips from this chapter that you think will help you the most, given your personal time management research. Write them below, with three corresponding actions that you will start tomorrow. For example, if you are going to set a strict schedule, three actions might be to establish the schedule, communicate it to your staff, and re-record your voicemail message.

1._____

    a._____

    b._____

    c._____

2._____

    a._____

    b._____

      c._____

3._____

      a._____

      b._____

      c._____

4._____

      a._____

      b._____

      c._____

Timesheet | Day One

Timeslot	Activities	More/Less/ Enough time?
7:00 – 7:30		
7:30 – 8:00		
8:00 – 8:30		
8:30 – 9:00		
9:00 – 9:30		
10:00 – 10:30		
10:30 – 11:00		
11:00 – 11:30		
11:30 – 12:00		
12:00 – 12:30		
12:30 – 1:00		
1:00 – 1:30		

1:30 – 2:00		
2:00 – 2:30		
2:30 – 3:00		
3:00 – 3:30		
3:30 – 4:00		
4:00 – 4:30		
4:30 – 5:00		
5:00 – 5:30		
5:30 – 6:00		
6:00 – 10:00 (Evening)		

Timesheet | Day Two

Timeslot	Activities	More/Less/ Enough time?
7:00 – 7:30		
7:30 – 8:00		
8:00 – 8:30		
8:30 – 9:00		
9:00 – 9:30		
10:00 – 10:30		
10:30 – 11:00		
11:00 – 11:30		
11:30 – 12:00		
12:00 – 12:30		
12:30 – 1:00		
1:00 – 1:30		

1:30 – 2:00		
2:00 – 2:30		
2:30 – 3:00		
3:00 – 3:30		
3:30 – 4:00		
4:00 – 4:30		
4:30 – 5:00		
5:00 – 5:30		
5:30 – 6:00		
6:00 – 10:00 (Evening)		

Timesheet | Day Three

Timeslot	Activities	More/Less/ Enough time?
7:00 – 7:30		
7:30 – 8:00		
8:00 – 8:30		
8:30 – 9:00		
9:00 – 9:30		
10:00 – 10:30		
10:30 – 11:00		
11:00 – 11:30		
11:30 – 12:00		
12:00 – 12:30		
12:30 – 1:00		
1:00 – 1:30		

1:30 – 2:00		
2:00 – 2:30		
2:30 – 3:00		
3:00 – 3:30		
3:30 – 4:00		
4:00 – 4:30		
4:30 – 5:00		
5:00 – 5:30		
5:30 – 6:00		
6:00 – 10:00 (Evening)		

Daily To-Do List | Business

Task	Priority (1-10)	Deadline?	Delegation?

Weekly To-Do List | Personal (Family, Leisure, etc.)

Task	Priority (1-10)	Deadline?	Delegation?

3

Define Your Target Market

What is a Target Market?

Many businesses can't answer the question: *Who is your target market?* They have often made the fatal assumption that *everyone* will want to purchase their product or service with the right marketing strategy.

A target market is simply the group of customers or clients who will, more likely than not, purchase a specific product or service. This group of people all have something in common. You need to determine what those characteristics are and how to reach them. It might be age, gender, social standing, geographic area, education level or what they do for entertainment.

Your target market, then, must be shown the value in purchasing that item or service from you. This includes both existing and potential customers, all of whom are motivated to do one of three things:

- Fulfill a need
- Solve a problem
- Satisfy a desire

To build, maintain, and grow your business, you need to know who your customers are, what they do, what they like, and why they would buy your product or service. Getting this wrong, or not taking the time to get it right, will cost you time, money, and potentially the success of your business.

The Importance of Knowing Your Target Market

Knowledge and understanding of your target market is the keystone in the arch of your business. Without it, your product or service positioning, pricing, marketing strategy, and eventually, your business could very quickly fall apart.

If you don't intimately know your target market, you run the risk of making mistakes when it comes to establishing pricing, product mix, or service packages. Your marketing strategy will lack direction and produce mediocre results at best. Even if your marketing message and unique selling proposition (USP) are clear, and your brochure is perfectly designed, it means nothing unless it arrives in the hands (or ears) of the right people.

Determining your target market takes time and careful diligence. While it often starts with a best guess, assumptions cannot be relied on and research is required to confirm original ideas. Your target market is not always your ideal market.

Once you build an understanding of who your target market is, keep up with your market research. Having your finger on the pulse of their motivations and drivers – which naturally change – will help you to anticipate needs or wants and evolve your business.

Types of Markets

Consumer

The Consumer Market includes those general consumers who buy products and services for personal use, or for use by family and friends. This is the market category you or I fall into when we're shopping for groceries or clothes, seeing a movie in the theatre, or going out for lunch. Retailers focus on this market category when marketing their goods or services.

Institutional

The Institutional Market serves society and provides products or services for the benefit of society. This includes hospitals, non-profit organizations, government organizations, schools and universities. Members of the Institutional Market purchase products to use in the provision of services to people in their care.

Business to Business (B2B)

The B2B Market is just what it seems to be; businesses that purchase the products and services of other business to run their operations. These purchases can include products that are used to manufacture other products (raw or technical), products that are needed for daily operations (such as office supplies), or services (such as accounting, shredding, and legal).

Reseller

This market can also be called the "Intermediary Market" because it consists of businesses that act as channels for goods and services between other markets. Goods are purchased and sold for a profit – without any alterations. Members of this market include wholesalers, retailers, resellers, and distributors.

Determining Your Target Market

Product / Service Investigation

The process for determining your target market starts by examining exactly what your offering is, and what the average customer's motivation for purchasing it is. Start by answering the following questions:

Does your offering meet a basic need?	
Does your offering serve a particular want?	
Does your offering fulfill a desire?	
What is the lifecycle of your product / service?	
What is the availability of your offering?	
What is the cost of the average customer's purchase?	
What is the lifecycle of your offering?	
How many times or how often will customers purchase your offering?	
Do you foresee any upcoming changes in your industry or region that may affect the sale of your offering (positive/negative)?	

Market Investigation

- **On the ground.** Spend some time on the ground researching who your target market might be. If you're thinking about opening a coffee shop, hang out in the neighborhood at different times of the day to get a sense of the people who live, work, and play in the neighborhood. Notice their age, gender, clothing, and any other indications of income and activities.

- **At the competition.** Who is your direct competitor targeting? Is there a small niche that is being missed? Observing the clientele of your competition can help to build understanding of your target market, regardless of whether it is the same or opposite. For example, if you own a children's clothing boutique and the majority of middle-class mothers shop at the local department store, you may wish to focus on higher-income families as your target market.

- **Online.** Many cities and towns, or at least regions, have demographic information available online. Research the ages, incomes, occupations, and other key pieces of information about the people who live in the area you operate your business. From this data, you will gain an understanding of the size of your total potential market.

- **With existing customers.** Talk to your existing customers through focus groups or surveys. This is a great way to gather demographic and behavioral information, as well as genuine feedback about product or service quality and other information that will be useful in a business or marketing strategy.

Who is Your Market?

Based on your product / service and market investigations, you will be able to piece together a basic picture of your target market, and some of their general characteristics. Record some notes here. At this point, you may wish to be as specific as possible, or maintain some generalities. You can further segment your market in the next section.

Consumer Target Market Framework

Market Type:	Consumer	
Gender:	☐ Male	☐ Female
Age Range:		
Purchase Motivation:	☐ Meet a Need ☐ Serve a Want ☐ Fulfill a Desire	
Activities:		
Income Range:		
Marital Status:		
Location:	☐ Neighborhood ☐ City ☐ Region ☐ Country	
Other Notes:		

Institutional Target Market Framework

Market Type:	Institutional	
Institution Type:	☐ Hospital ☐ Non-profit ☐ School ☐ University ☐ Charity ☐ Government ☐ Church	
Purchase Motivation:	☐ Operational Need ☐ Client Want ☐ Client Desire	
Purpose of Institution:		
Size:		
Location:	☐ Neighborhood ☐ City ☐ Region ☐ Country	

Other Notes:	

B2B Target Market Framework

Market Type:	Business to Business (B2B)
Company Size:	
Number of Employees:	
Purchase Motivation:	☐ Operations Need ☐ Strategy ☐ Functionality
Annual Revenue:	
Industry:	
Location(s):	
Purpose of Business:	
People, Culture & Values:	

Other Notes:	

Reseller Target Market Framework

Market Type:	Reseller
Industry:	
Client Base:	
Purchase Motivation:	☐ Operations Need ☐ Client Wants ☐ Functionality
Annual Revenue:	

Age:	
Location:	☐ Neighborhood ☐ City ☐ Region ☐ Country
Other Notes:	

Your Target Market: Putting It Together

Based on the information you gather from your product / service and market investigations; you should have a clear vision of your realistic target market. Here are a few examples of how this information is put together and conclusions are drawn:

Target Market Sample 1: Consumer Market

Business: Baby Clothing Boutique	**Business Purpose:** *Meet a need* (provide clothing for infants and children aged 0 to 5 years) *Serve a want* (clothing is brand name only, and has a higher price point than the competition)
Market Type: Consumer	
Gender: Women	
Marital Status: Married	
Market Observations: Located on Main Street of Anytown. A street that is seeing many new boutiques opening. Close proximate to the main shopping mall and two blocks from a popular mid-range restaurant that is busy at lunch	**Industry Predictions:** Large number of new housing developments in the city and surrounding areas. Two new schools under construction and they expect to see an influx of new families move to town.

Competition Observations: Baby clothing also available at two local department stores, and one second-hand shop on opposite side of town.	**Online Research:** Half of Anytown's population is female, and 25% have children under the age of 15 years. Anytown's population is expected to increase by 32% within three years. The average household income for Anytown is $75,000 annually

TARGET MARKET:

The target market can then be described as married mothers with children under five years old, between the ages of 25 and 45, who have recently moved to Anytown from Anycity, and have a household income of at least $100K annually.

Target Market Sample 2: B2B Market

Business: Confidential Paper Shredding	**Target Business Size:** Small to medium
Market Type: B2B (Business to Business)	**Target Business Revenue:** $500K to $1M
Business Purpose: *Meet an operations need* (provide confidential on-site shredding services for business documents)	**Target Business Type:** Produce or handle a variety of sensitive paper documentation; accountants, lawyers, real estate agents, etc.
Market Observations: There are two main areas of office buildings and industrial warehouses in Anycity, three more office towers are being constructed and will be completed this year.	**Industry Predictions:** The professional sector is seeing revenue growth of 24% over last year, which indicates increased client billing and staff recruitment

Competition Observations: One confidential shredding company serves the region, covering Anycity and the surrounding towns. They provide regular (weekly or biweekly) service, but do not have the capacity to handle large volumes at one time.	**Online Research:** Anycity's biggest employment sectors are: manufacturing, tourism, food services, and professional services

TARGET MARKET:

The target market can then be described as small to medium sized businesses in the professional sector with an annual revenue of $500K to $1M who require both regular and infrequent large volume paper shredding services.

Segmenting Your Market

Your market segments are the groups within your target market, broken down by a determinant in one of the following four categories:

- Demographic
- Psychographic
- Geographic
- Behavior

Segmenting your target market into several more specific groups allows you to further tailor your marketing campaign and more specifically position your product or service. You may wish to divide your ad campaign into four sections, and target four specific markets with messages that will most resonate with the audience.

For example, the baby clothing store may choose to segment its target market by psychographics, or lifestyle. If the larger target market is *married females with children under five, between the ages of 25 and 45, who have a household income of at least $100K annually*, it can be broken down into the following lifestyle segments:

- Fitness-oriented mothers
- Career-oriented mothers
- New mothers

With these three categories, unique marketing messages can be created that speak to the hot buttons of each segment. The more accurate and specific you can make communications with your target market, the greater impact you will have on your revenues.

Market Segmentation Variables

Demographic	Psychographic	Geographic	Behavioristic
Age	Personality	Region	Brand Loyalty
Income	Lifestyle	Country	Product Usage
Gender	Values	City	Purchase
Generation	Attitude	Area	Frequency
Nationality	Motivation	Neighborhood	Profitability
Ethnicity	Activities	Density	Readiness to Buy
Marital Status	Interests	Climate	User Status
Family Size			
Occupation			
Religion			
Language			
Education			
Employment Type			
Housing Type			
Housing Ownership			
Political			

Understanding Your Target Market

Once you have determined who your market is, make a point of learning everything you can about them. You need to have a strong understanding of who they are, what they like, where they shop, why they buy, and how they spend their time. Remind yourself that you may *think* you know your market, but until you have verified the information, you'll be driving your marketing strategy blind.

Also be aware that markets change, just like people. Just because you knew your market when you started your business 10 years ago, doesn't mean you know it now. Regular market research is part of any successful business plan, and a great habit to start.

Types of Market Research

Surveys

The simplest way to gather information from your clients or target market is through a survey. You can craft a questionnaire full of questions about your product, service, market demographics, buyer motivations, and so on. Plus, anonymous surveys will produce the most accurate information since names are not attached to the results or specific comments.

Depending on the purpose—whether it is to gather demographic information, product or service feedback, or other data—there are several ways to administer a survey.

1. Telephone

Telephone surveys are a more time-consuming option but have the benefit of live communication with your target market. Generally, it is best to have a third party conduct this type of survey to gather the most honest feedback. This is the method that market researchers use for polling, which is highly reliable.

2. Online

Online surveys are the easiest to administer yourself. There a many web-based services that quickly and easily allow you to custom create your survey and send it to your email marketing list. These services can also analyze, summarize and interpret the results on your behalf. Keep in mind that the results include only those who are motivated to respond, which may sway your results.

3. Paper-based.

Paper surveys are seldom used and can prove to be an inefficient method. Like online surveys, your results are based on the feedback of those who were motivated for one reason or another to respond. The time and effort involved in taking the survey, filing it out, and returning it to your place of business may deter people from participating.

Keep in mind that surveys can be complex to administer and consume more time and resources than you have planned. If you have the budget, consider hiring a professional market research firm to lead or assist with the process. This will also ensure that the methodology is standard practice and will garner the most accurate results.

Website Analysis

Tracking your website traffic is an excellent way to research your existing and potential customer's interests and behavior. From this information, you can ensure the design, structure and content of your website is catering to the people who use it and the people you want to use it.

User-friendly website traffic analytics programs can easily show you who is visiting your site, where they are from, and what pages of your site they are viewing. Services like Google Analytics can tell you what page they arrive at, where they click to, how much time they spend on each page, and on which page they leave the site.

This is powerful (and free!) information to have in your market research, and easy to monitor monthly or weekly, depending on the needs of your business.

Customer Purchase Data (Consumer Behavior)

If you do not have the budget to conduct your own professional market research, you can use existing resources on consumer behavior. While this data may not be specific to your region or city, general consumer research is actual data that can be helpful in confirming assumptions you may have made about your target market.

Your customer loyalty program or Point of Sale system may also be of help in tracking customer purchases and identifying trends in purchase behavior. If you can track who is buying, what they're buying and how often they're buying, you'll have an arsenal of powerful insight into your existing client base.

Focus Groups

Focus groups look at the psychographic and behavioristic aspects of your target market. Groups of six to 12 people are gathered and asked general and specific questions about their purchase motivations and behaviors. These questions could relate to your particular business, or to the general industry.

Focus group sessions can also be time consuming to organize and facilitate, so consider hiring the services of a professional market research firm. You may also receive more honest information if a third party is asking the questions and receiving the responses from focus group participants.

For cost savings, consider partnering with an associate in the same industry who is not a direct competitor, and who would benefit from the same market data.

4

Creating a Powerful Offer

I'm not going to beat around the bush on this one:

Your offer is the granite foundation of your marketing campaign.

Get it right, and everything else will fall into place. Your headline will grab readers, your copy will sing, your ad layout will hardly matter, and you will have customers running to your door.

Get it wrong, and even the best looking, best-written campaign will sink like the Titanic. A powerful offer is an irresistible offer. It's an offer that gets your audience frothing at the mouth and clamoring over each other all the way to your door. An offer that makes your readers pick up the phone and open their wallets.

Irresistible offers make your potential customers think, "I'd be crazy not to take him up on that," or "An offer like this doesn't come around very often." They instill a sense of emotion, of desire, and ultimately, urgency.

Make it easy for customers to purchase from you the first time, and spend your time keeping them coming back.

I'll say it again: **get it right, and everything else will fall into place.**

The Crux of Your Marketing Campaign

As you work your way through this program, you will find that nearly every chapter discusses the importance of a powerful offer as related to your marketing strategy or promotional campaign.

There's a reason for this. The powerful offer is the reason a customer will open their wallets. It is how you generate leads, and then convert them into loyal customers. The more dramatic, unbelievable, and valuable the offer is the more dramatic and unbelievable the response will be. Many companies spend thousands of dollars on impressive marketing campaigns in glossy magazines and big city newspapers. They send massive direct mail campaigns on a regular basis; yet don't receive an impressive or massive response rate.

These companies do not yet understand that simply providing information on their company and the benefits of their product is not enough to get customers to act. There is no reason to pick up the phone or visit the store, *right now*.

Your powerful, irresistible offer can:
- Increase leads
- Drive traffic to your website or business
- Move old product
- Convert leads into customers
- Build your customer database

What Makes a Powerful Offer?

A powerful offer is one that makes the most people respond and act. It gets people running to spend money on your product or service.

56

Powerful offers nearly always have an element of *urgency* and of *scarcity*. They give your audience a reason to act immediately, instead of putting it off until a later date.

Urgency relates to time. The offer is only available until a certain date, during a certain period of the day, or if you act within a few hours of seeing the ad. The customer needs to act now to take advantage of the offer.

Scarcity related to quantity. There are only a certain number of customers who will be able to take advantage of the offer. There may be a limited number of spaces, a limited number of products, or simply a limited number of people the business will provide the offer to. Again, this requires that customer acts immediately to reap the high value for low cost.

Powerful offers also:

Offer great value. Customers perceive the offer as having great value. It is more than a single product on its own, or the product at its regular price. It is clear that the offer takes the reader's needs and wants into consideration.

Make sense to the reader. They are simple and easy to understand if read quickly. Avoid percentages. Use half off or 2 for 1 instead of 50% off. There are no "catches" or requirements; no fine print.

Seems logical. The offer doesn't come out of thin air. There is a logical reason behind it; a holiday, end of season, anniversary celebration, or new product. People can get suspicious of offers that seem "too good to be true" and have no apparent purpose.

Provide a premium. The offer provides something extra to the customer, like a free gift, or free product or service. They feel they are getting something extra for no extra cost. Premiums are perceived to have more value than discounts.

Remember that when your target market reads your offer, they will be asking the following questions:

1. What are you offering me?
2. What's in it for me?
3. What makes me sure I can believe you?
4. How much do I have to pay for it?

The Most Powerful Types of Offers

Decide what kind of offer will most effectively achieve your objectives. Are you trying to generate leads, convert customers, build a database, move old product off the shelves, or increase sales? Consider what type of offer will be of most value to your ideal customer and what will make them act quickly.

Free Offer

This type of offer asks customers to act immediately in exchange for something free. This is a good strategy to use to build a customer database or mailing list. Offer a free consultation, free consumer report, or other item of low cost to you but of high perceived value.

You can also advertise the value of the item you are offering for free. For example, act now and you'll receive a free consultation worth $75 dollars. This will dramatically increase your lead generation and allow you to focus on conversion when the customer comes through the door or picks up the phone.

The Value-Added Offer

Add additional services or products that cost you very little and combine them with other items to increase their attractiveness. This increases the perception of value in the customer's mind, which will justify increasing the price of a product or service without incurring extra hard costs to your business.

Bundling

Package your products or services together in a logical way to increase the perceived value as a whole. Discount the value of the package by a small margin and position it as a "start-up kit" or "special package." By packaging goods of mixed values, you will be able to close more high-value sales. For example: including a free desk-jet printer with every computer purchase.

Premium Offer

Offer a bonus product or service with the purchase of another. This strategy will serve your bottom line much better than discounting. This includes 2 for 1 offers, offers that include free gifts, and in-store credit with purchases over a specific dollar amount.

Urgency Offer

As I mentioned above, offers that include an element of urgency enjoy a better response rate, as there is a reason for your customers to act immediately. Give the offer a deadline or limit the number of spots available.

Guarantee Offer

Offer to take the risk of making a purchase away from your customers. Guarantee the performance or results of your product or service and offer to compensate the customer with their money back if they are not satisfied. This will help overcome any fear or reservations about your product and make it more likely for your leads to become customers.

Create Your Powerful Offer

1. Pick a single product or service.

Focus on only one product or service, or one product or service type at a time. This will keep your offer clear, simple, and easy to understand. This can be an area of your business you wish to grow, or old product that you need to move off the shelves.

2. Decide what you want your customers to do.

What are you looking to achieve from your offer? If it is to generate more leads, then you'll need your customer to contact you. If it is to quickly sell old product, you'll need your customer to come into the store and buy it. Do you want them to visit your website? Sign up for your newsletter? How long do they have to act? Be clear about your call to action, and state it clearly in your offer.

3. Dream up the biggest, best offer.

First, think of the biggest, best things you could offer your customers, regardless of cost and ability. Don't limit yourself to a single type of offer, combine several types of offers to increase value. Offer a premium, plus a guarantee, with a package offer. Then, take a look at what you've created and make the necessary changes, so it is realistic.

4. Run the numbers.

Finally, make sure the offer will leave you with some profit. You don't want to publish an outrageous offer that will generate a tremendous number of leads, but leave you broke. Remember that each customer has an acquisition cost, as well as a lifetime value. The amount of their first purchase may allow you to break even, but the amount of their subsequent purchases may make you a lovely profit. Businesses fail the quickest when they do not know their numbers

5

How to Use Testimonials and Profit
from Social Proof

The Power of Testimonials

Testimonials are simply the single most powerful asset you can have in your marketing toolkit. When your customers tell others about the benefits of choosing your business, it is a thousand times more powerful than the same words from your mouth.

The words and opinions of others motivate people to spend money every day. From celebrity endorsements on TV and in magazines, to casual conversations with friends, decisions about what product or service to buy and what brand or provider to use, are heavily influenced by those who have purchased before. Why? Many people have an inherent distrust of salespeople, and a skepticism toward marketing materials. Others are bombarded with choices and are looking for some sense of security in their purchase decision.

Testimonials build the credibility of your business, break down natural barriers, and create a sense of trust for the consumer. They have an incredible ability to persuade customers to buy, and to buy from you. Think about the last time someone recommended a brand of laundry detergent, a bottle of wine, or a plumber to you. Their positive experience had more of an impact on your decision to buy than any advertisement or discount.

When it comes to spending money, people want a sure bet. They want to know that someone else has bought before, and they want to know that the product or service has delivered the promised results. A testimonial for your business is worth more than any copywriter, clever ad slogan, or sales pitch.

Customers Who Give Testimonials

When people put their name and reputation on paper to endorse something, it creates a sense of loyalty. If questioned, they will back their decision, even if they find later their decision was wrong.

When someone is willing to endorse your product or service in writing, they have likely already started a word-of-mouth chain of verbal testimonials about their positive experience. Remember the last time you discovered a chiropractic miracle worker? Or the fastest and cheapest drycleaner? Didn't you tell every one of your friends who could use the service?

By asking a customer for a testimonial, you are asking for their assistance in the growth of your business. When they feel they are truly helping and participating in the development of your company, their sense of pride will mean continuous loyalty to your product or service.

11 Ways to Get Great Testimonials

Testimonials are powerful – no question. But how do you make sure that the quotes you get from your customers will bring you the most value? How do you ensure that your client will articulate your product's merits in a clear and easy to understand way that you can actually use in your marketing materials?

Asking for testimonials requires more effort than merely soliciting general comments and praise. You want to ensure that your customer feels a sense of pride and loyalty in providing their opinion, and that their opinion will have an impact on potential buyers.

Here are 11 proven ways to get great testimonials from your customers.

1. Don't wait!

Your customers are the happiest and most willing to help you within a day or two of their purchase, so aim to secure the testimonial in this time period. Ask for the testimonial before they leave, and make sure you have all their contact details to follow up with. This also ensures you stay on top of your testimonial recruitment!

2. Get specific

Specific testimonials are more believable. The more specific you can have your customer be, the stronger and more impactful the testimonial will be. Meaningful details get remembered. Ask for them to mention things like time, dates, extraordinary customer service, and personal observations. Don't forget to have them mention when they were there.

3. If you were the solution – what was the problem?

Testimonials that tell stories are more engaging. Ask client to not only describe their experience with your company, but also the negative experience that led them to your door. If they can describe the struggles and challenges, they were facing before receiving your service, the reader will likely be able to sympathize and resonate with similar struggles. This will motivate them to solve their problems with your solution.

4. Write the first draft

Make it easy for your clients. This technique is something you can offer someone who is hesitant to commit to writing a testimonial due to time constraints or is procrastinating. Ask them to brainstorm a few notes they would like to include in their feedback, write them down, and string them into a concise testimonial for their review. All they have to do is review, print on their letterhead, sign, and mail back to you!

5. Include your marketing message or USP

Always ask your customers to include your unique selling proposition (USP) in the testimonial. For instance, if your USP includes exceptional customer service, same-day installation, and a money-back guarantee then ask your customer to attest to those qualities.

6. A picture says...

Yes, you know the saying. But it's true. When readers attach an image of the speaker to words, the words are enlivened and have twice as much validity and impact. When readers see an image of a previous client using your product or service, their words and opinions are even more believable. And most customers like to see themselves!

7. Credentials equal trust

As we mentioned, testimonials from credible sources will have the most believability and impact. When you ask for a testimonial, make sure your customer states their expertise and credentials. If you sell custom orthotics, and can secure a solid testimonial from a doctor, their words will be golden in your marketing materials.

8. Don't forget to ask permission

When you ask for testimonials, make sure you are clear that their words may be used in your marketing materials, including advertisements, website and in-store displays. This is a good time to thank them for their time and sincerity and show your appreciation for their words.

9. Location, location...

Depending on the market reach of your business, the location of your customers is an important part of the believability of your testimonial. If you own a community-based business, when potential clients see you've made others happy just down their street, they'll be motivated to use your service too. If you own a regional business, then the cities and addresses of other happy customers can help communicate the reach of your service.

10. Testimonials are not surveys

Keep the purpose of your request in mind when you're asking for testimonials. Testimonials should be positive fodder for your advertising materials. Surveys are used to solicit meaningful (and often confidential) customer information to refine and improve your service. Testimonials are public statements, while surveys are often anonymous and can produce less-than-positive results.

11. Say thank you!

Thanking a customer for their time and effort creating your testimonial is just plain good manners. It also increases loyalty and goodwill. This can be done via email but sending a formal letter on your letterhead, is a more meaningful approach. And always remember to hand write their name and address.

Using Testimonials Strategically

So now you have a pile of glowing customer testimonials. What's next?

Choose the most powerful piece of the testimonial

What is the most convincing aspect of the testimonial? Is it the author? Where they are from? A specific sentence or paragraph they wrote? Be strategic about the aspect of the testimonial that you feature and select what will have the most impact.

For example, you can compile a list titled *What Customers are Saying*, and list only the phrases that support your specific marketing message. Or you can feature the unique credentials or story of your customer, before you even include their testimonial. You can also summarize the testimonial with a powerful headline.

Put them on your website

Adding a page of testimonials to your website is a great start, especially when you're beginning to solicit customer responses. However, the most powerful way to ensure site visitors actually see your testimonials is to include them on every page. Especially the ones with the highest traffic! Get enough testimonials so your web site can rotate through them.

A testimonial should be placed wherever you make a strong statement about your service or product, and wherever the service or product is described. This is a great way to break up your sales copy with some "proof". As they read about your offering, your credibility will be validated by someone other than you.

Compile your best 25 to 50 letters in a display book

Like a proud grandparent, keep a book of testimonials in the waiting area of your office, your boardroom, and in your desk. Or, put one at the service counter, cash register and anywhere else people may have a moment to flip through.

I've seen this done in recruiting firm, a hardware store, and a physiotherapist's office. When clients have a chance to read the positive experiences of others, they will be more open to hearing your sales pitch less guarded when responding to your unique offering.

Hang your favorite testimonials in your store or office

Testimonials as art! Frame your favorite testimonials, preferably the ones written on client letterhead, and post them on the wall in your business. Even if clients don't read them up close, the volume and visual recognition of client logos will have impact. Plus, your next satisfied clients will want to see their company names on the wall too.

Put them in your advertisements

Use short, clear, concise testimonials in your advertising. When was the last time you saw a prescription drug advertisement without a testimonial? Can't remember? That's because you haven't. The best advertisers know that testimonials are the fastest and most effective way to overcome skepticism and get clients thinking that your product or service is the solution to their problem.

Include a page of testimonials in your direct mail

When sending your marketing materials directly to a mass list of potential clients, let the words of others speak to the merits of your product or service. Put together a page or two of testimonials and attach it to your mailing. The credibility of your company will be instantly established, encouraging clients to act and buy faster.

Partner with an associate for joint mailing

If you have an associate or colleague who has a similar customer base of new prospects for your business, try a joint-endorsed mailing. Each of you will send a letter to your own clients, endorsing the other's products and services. Your service or solution is offered to a potential client by a trusted source, and you are offering your existing clients the added value of an associate's service to complement your own.

Testimonial Request Letter

Here is an example of a basic testimonial request letter that can be customized and made into a template for your unique business. This can also be sent over email if that is how your clients prefer to be contacted.

Mr. John Smith
1234 Main Street
Anytown, Anyplace 90210   *January 2, 2006*

Dear Mr. Smith,

Thank you for visiting our store this week. It was a pleasure helping you select a new laptop for your daughter to use at university this fall. They just grow up too fast! Your research and clear idea of the product you were searching for truly made our job easy. We love the back to school season, because it means working with clients like yourself.

We know there are a lot of choices when it comes to purchasing a laptop, so thank you for choosing ABC Company. If there is anything else we can assist you with, please don't hesitate to contact me directly.

We occasionally ask select customers for their feedback in the form of a testimonial. Because we are so proud of the feedback we receive, we often use our customer's quotes in our marketing materials – specifically our website and sales brochures. The real-life experiences of our customers at ABC Company are stories that we are proud of.

Could I ask you to write down some of your feedback? A few words about your experience with ABC Company, and how we helped you and your daughter would be greatly appreciated. We encourage you to print this on your company letterhead, so we can provide your own company with some exposure as well.

You may want to include the names of the associates who helped you, and how your daughter is enjoying her laptop. Again, we would like to feature your name and experience in our marketing materials. For your convenience, I've included a prepaid envelope with which to mail your testimonial back to us.

Thank you very much for your assistance.

Kind regards,

Your name here

Testimonial Thank You Letter

Here is an example of a short thank you letter for a testimonial that can also be customized and made into a template for your unique business. You may wish to write r thank you letters on company note cards, but try to avoid sending these via email.

Mr. John Smith
1234 Main Street
Anytown, Anyplace 90210   *January 10, 2006*

Dear Mr. Smith,

We received your glowing testimonial in the mail today, and I wanted to thank you personally for your kind words. Your comments about our store and our people are important to us, and I will make sure my staff takes a moment to read your letter.

We are thrilled that your daughter is enjoying her laptop and using it to keep in touch with you while she studies abroad. When we sold it to you, we truly believed it would provide the most long-lasting value for her student budget. I hope it serves her for the rest of her time at school.

Thank you again for taking the time to write us. We are all proud to have been of service to you and your daughter and look forward to seeing you both again soon.

Warm regards,

Your Name Here

Testimonial Examples

Below you will find a series of sample testimonials, and excerpts from testimonial letters. Read these over and take a moment to notice why each is a powerful statement. I have also summarized each testimonial with a headline.

24% Response Rate from a Single Direct Mailing!

We were skeptical about direct mail campaigns, and unsure about the return on investment. Your strategic advice and logistical help made the project run smoothly. We received over 200 leads from this one effort!

John and Betty McFee
Scottsdale, AZ

Best Sleep in 20 Years!

I can't tell you how much I appreciated Craig's patience and assistance in my mattress selection. He is so knowledgeable of each mattress' design and features and helped us find a financing solution that worked with our budget. I haven't slept this well in over two decades. Promote him!

Jason Carmichael

Gentle and effective approach

I have always been reluctant to visit a chiropractor for my lower back pain because I am not comfortable with physical adjustments. Sarah took the time to clearly explain the cause of my pain and gave me easy exercises to help correct the problem. She respected my comfort level and treated me without uncomfortable cracks and snaps!

Wally Orton

Testimonial Worksheet

Start today! Brainstorm a list of recent customers and clients who you will approach for testimonials. Post this worksheet in your office and track your progress. Aim for 50 testimonials in two months. You can never have too many.

Name + Phone	Request Letter Sent	Follow Up Call Made	Testimonial Received	Thank-you Letter Sent
	☐	☐	☐	☐
	☐	☐	☐	☐
	☐	☐	☐	☐
	☐	☐	☐	☐
	☐	☐	☐	☐
	☐	☐	☐	☐
	☐	☐	☐	☐
	☐	☐	☐	☐
	☐	☐	☐	☐
	☐	☐	☐	☐
	☐	☐	☐	☐
	☐	☐	☐	☐
	☐	☐	☐	☐
	☐	☐	☐	☐

	☐	☐	☐	☐
	☐	☐	☐	☐
	☐	☐	☐	☐
	☐	☐	☐	☐

6

Immediate Sales

If you're a business owner, you're also a salesperson.

You've had to sell the bank to get them to loan you your start-up capital. You've had to sell the best employees on why they should work for your business. You've had to convince your business partner, spouse, and friends why your business idea is a good one. Now you must repeatedly sell your product or service to your customers.

The ability to sell effectively and efficiently is one every successful business owner has cultivated and continues to develop. It can be a complicated and time-consuming task; one that you will have to continually work on throughout your career in order to be and stay successful.

Fortunately, making sales is a step-by-step process that can be learned, customized, and continuously improved. There are a wide range of tools available to help and support your sales efforts.

You don't have to be the most outgoing, enthusiastic person to be successful at sales. You don't even have to be a good public speaker. All you need is an understanding of the basic sales process, and a genuine passion for what you are selling.

Sales 101

As I said before, making sales is a process. There are clear, step-by-step actions that can be taken and result in a sale. The sales process varies according to the type of business, type of customer and the type of product or service that is offered; however, the core steps are the same. Similarly, sales training varies from individual to individual, but the core skills and abilities remain the same.

Here is a basic seven-step process that you can follow, or fine tune to suit your unique products and services. Remember that each step is important and builds on the step previous. It is essential to become adept at each step, instead of solely focusing on closing the sale.

1. Preparation

Make sure you have prepared for your meeting, presentation, or day on the sales floor. You have complete control of this part of the sales process, so it is important to do everything you can to set the stage for your success.

- Understand your product or service inside and out.
- Prepare all the necessary materials and organize them neatly.
- Keep your place of business tidy and organized. Reface any product on the shelves.
- Ensure you appear professional and well groomed.
- Do some research on your potential client and brainstorm to find common ground.

2. Build a Relationship

The first few minutes you spend with a potential customer set the stage for the rest of your interaction. First impressions are everything. Your goal in the second step is to relax the customer and begin to develop a relationship with them. Establishing a real relationship with your customer will create trust.

- Make a great first impression: shake hands, make eye contact, and introduce yourself.
- Remain confident and professional, but also personable.
- Mirror their speech and behavior.
- Begin with general questions and small talk.
- Show interest in them and their place of business.
- Notice and comment on positives.
- Find some common ground on which to relate.
- Talk more about them and less about you.

3. Discuss Needs and Wants

Once you have spent a few moments getting to know your prospect, start asking open-ended questions to discover some of their needs and wants. If they have come to you on the sales floor, ask what brought them in the store. If you are meeting them to present your product or service, ask why they are interested in, or what criteria they have in mind for that product or service.

- If you are making a sales presentation, ask for a few moments at the outset to outline the purpose of your visit, as well as how you have structured the presentation.

- Listen intently and repeat back information you are not sure you understand.
- Ask open-ended questions to get them talking. The longer they talk, the more insight they are providing you into their needs and purchase motivations.
- Ask clarifying questions about their responses.
- If you become sure the customer is going to buy your product or service, begin to ask questions specific to the offering. i.e., what size/color do you prefer?

4. Present the Solution

Every customer has a problem they do not want and a solution they do not have. Once you have a solid understanding of what they are looking for, or what issue they are looking to resolve, you can begin to present the solution: your product or service.

- Explain how your product or service will solve their problem or meet their needs. If several products apply, begin by presenting the mid-level product.
- Illustrate your points with anecdotes about other happy customers or awards the product or service has earned.
- Use hypothetical examples featuring your customer. Encourage them to picture a scenario after their purchase.
- Begin by describing the benefits of the product, then follow up with features and advantages.
- Watch your customer's behavior as you speak and ask further qualifying questions in response to body language and verbal comments.

- Give the customer an opportunity to ask you questions or provide feedback about each product or service after you have described or explained it.
- Ask closed-ended questions to gain agreement.

5. Overcome Objections

As you present the product or service, take note of potential objections by asking open-ended questions and monitoring body language. Expect that objections will arise and prepare for it. Consider brainstorming a list of all potential objections and writing down your responses.

- Repeat the objection back to the customer to ensure you understand them correctly.
- Empathize with what they have said, and then provide a response that overcomes the objection.
- Confirm that the answer you have provided has overcome their objection by repeating yourself.

The Eight Most Common Objections
The product or service does not seem valuable to me. There is no reason for me to act know. I will wait. It's safest not to make a decision right away. There is not enough money for the purchase. The competitor or another department offers a better product. There are internal issues between people or departments. The relationship with the decision maker is strained. There is an existing contract in place with another business.

6. Close

This is an important part of the sales process that should be handled delicately. Deciding when to close is a judgment call that must be made in the moment during the sale. Ideally, you have presented a solution to their problem, overcome objections, and have the customer in a place where they are ready to buy.

Here are some questions to ask before you close the sale:

- Does my prospect agree that there is value in my product or service?
- Does my prospect understand the features and benefits of the product or service?
- Are there any remaining objections that must be handled?
- What other factors could influence my prospect's decision to buy?
- Have I minimized the risk involved in the purchase, and provided some level of urgency?

Once you have determined it is time to make the sale, here are some sample statements you can use to get the process rolling:

- So, should we get started?
- Shall I grab a new one from the back?
- If you just give me your credit card, I can take care of the transaction while you continue browsing.
- When would you like the product delivered?
- We can begin next month if we receive payment by the end of the week.
- Can I email you a draft contract tomorrow?

7. Service and Follow-up

Once you have made the sale, your work is not over. You want to ensure that that customer will become a loyal, repeat customer, and that they will refer their friends to your business.

Ask them to be in your customer database and keep in touch with regular newsletters. Follow up with a phone call or drop by to ask how they are enjoying the product or service, and if they have any further questions or needs you can assist them with. This contact opportunity will also allow you ask for a referral, or an up sell. At the very least, it will ensure you are continuing to foster and build a relationship with the client.

Up-selling

Up-selling is simply inviting your customers to spend more money in your business by purchasing additional products or services. This could include more of the same product, complementary products, or impulse items. 34% of people asked will purchase additional products or services.

Up-selling is an effective way to increase profits and create loyal clients, without spending any money to acquire the business. These clients are already purchasing from you. They already perceive value in what you have to offer, so take the information you have gained in the sales process and offer them a little bit more.

You experience up-selling on a daily basis. From "do you want fries with that?" to "have you heard about our product protect program?" companies across the globe have tapped into and trained their staff on the value of the up sell.

Up selling is truly rooted in good customer service. If your client purchases a new computer printer, you'll need to make sure they have the cords required to connect it to the computer, regular and photo paper, and color and black and white ink. If you don't suggest these items, they may arrive home and realize they do not have all the materials needed to use the product. They may choose to purchase those materials somewhere closer, cheaper, or more helpful.

Customer education is another form of up-selling. What if you customer doesn't realize that you sell a variety of printer paper and stationery in addition to computer hardware like printers? Take every opportunity to educate your customer on the products and services you offer that may be of interest to them.

An effective way of implementing an up-sell system into your business is simply by creating add-on checklists for the products or services you offer. Each item has a list of related items that your customer may need. This will encourage your staff to develop the habit of asking for the up sell.

Other up sell strategies can be implemented:

- **At the point of sale**. This is a great place for impulse items like candy, flashlights, nail scissors, etc.
- **In a newsletter**. This is an effective strategy for customer education.
- **In your merchandising**. Place strips of impulse items near related items. For example, paper clips with paper and pens near binders.
- **Over the phone**. If someone is placing an order for delivery, offer additional items in the same shipment for convenience.
- **With new products**. Feature each new product or service that you offer prominently in your business and ask your staff to mention it to every customer.

Sales Team

What Makes a Good Salesperson?

There are a lot of salespeople out there. But what qualities and skills make a great salesperson? These are the attributes you will want to find or develop in your team:

- Willingness to continuously learn and improve sales skills
- Sincerity in relating to customers and providing solutions to their objectives
- An understanding of the company's big picture
- A communication style that is direct, polite, and professional
- Honesty and respect for other team members, customers, as well as the competition.
- Ability to manage time
- Enthusiastic
- Inquisitive
- A great listener
- Ability to quickly interpret, analyze, and respond to information during the sales process
- Ability to connect and develop relationships of trust with potential clients
- Professional appearance

Team Building — Keeping Your Team Together

In many businesses, sales is an entire department or a whole team of people who work together to generate leads and convert customers. Effective management of your sales team is a skill every business owner should cultivate.

Teambuilding, recruitment, and training will be discussed in later sections, but take some time to consider the following aspects of managing a sales team:

Communication

- Are targets and results regularly reviewed?
- Are opportunities for input regularly provided?
- Do sales staff members have a clear understanding of what is expected?
- Do all staff members know daily, weekly, and quarterly targets?

Performance Management

- Are sales staff members motivated to reach targets?
- Are sales staff recognized and rewarded once those targets are reached?
- Are there opportunities for skills training and development?
- Do staff members have broad and comprehensive product or industry knowledge?
- Is there opportunity for growth within the company?
- Is performance regularly reviewed?

Operations

- Do you have a solid understanding of your sales numbers (revenue, profit, margins)?

- Are your sales processes regularly reviewed?
- Do you have a variety of sales scripts prepared?
- Do you measure conversion rates?
- How are your leads generated?

Sales Tools

Every salesperson should have an arsenal of tools on hand to assist them in the sales process. These tools can act as aids while a sale is taking place or help to foster continual learning and development of the salesperson's skills and approach.

The list below includes some popular sales tools. Add to this list with other resources that are specific to your business or industry.

Tool	Description and Benefit
Scripts	Used for incoming and outgoing telemarketing, cold calls, door-to-door sales, in-store sales Create several different scripts throughout your business Maintains consistency in your sales approach Revise and renew your scripts regularly
Presentation Materials	High-quality information about your product or service Forms: PowerPoint presentation, brochure, product sheets, proposal Serves as an outline of your sales presentation, and keeps you on task
Colleagues	A source of help and advice, especially when you are on the same team or sell similar products They are also a source of support.

Customer Databases	An accurate, up-to-date database of customer contact information and contact history Used to stay in touch with clients Can also be used for direct mail and follow-up telemarketing
The Internet	A powerful resource for sales help and advice Information to help improve your sales process Online sales coaching Source for product knowledge
Ongoing Training	Constant improvement of your sales skills Constant increase in product knowledge Investment in yourself and your company

8 Tips for Better Sales

- **Dress for the sale.** Dress professionally, appear well put together and maintain good hygiene. Ensure you are not only dressed professionally, but *appropriately*. Would your client feel more comfortable if you wore a suit, or jeans and blazer?

- **Speak their language.** Show you understand their industry or culture and use phrases your customer understands. This may require researching industry jargon or common phrases. Remember to avoid using words and phrases that are used in the sales process: sold, contract, telemarketing, finance, interest, etc. Doing so will help break down the salesperson/customer barrier.

- **Ooze positivity**. Show up or answer the phone with a smile and leave your personal or business issues behind. Be enthusiastic about what you have to offer, and how that offering will benefit your customer. Reflect this not only in your voice, but also in your body language.

- **Deliver a strong pitch or presentation**. Be confident and convincing. Leave self-doubt at the door and walk in assuming the sale. Take time to explain complex concepts, and always connect what you're saying to your audience in a specific way.

- **Be a poster child for good manners**. Accept any amenity you're offered, listen intently, don't interrupt, don't show up late, have a strong handshake, and give everyone you are speaking to equal attention.

- **Avoid sensitive subjects**. Politics, religion, swearing, sexual innuendos and racial comments are absolutely off-limits. So are negative comments about other customers or the competition.

- **Create a real relationship.** Icebreakers and small talk are not just to pass the time before your presentation. They are how relationships get established. Show genuine interest in everything your customer has to say. Ask questions about topics you know they are passionate. Speak person to person, not salesperson to customer. Remember everything.

- **Know more than you need to.** Impress clients with comprehensive knowledge – not only of your product or service – but also of the people who use that product or service, and industry trends. Be seen as an expert in order to build trust and respect.

7

How to Create Repeat Business and Have Clients that Pay, Stay and Refer

When it comes to marketing and generating more income, most business owners are focused outward.

They've carefully established and segmented their target market and created specific offers and messages for each market segment. They spend thousands of dollars in advertising and direct mail campaigns in hot pursuit of more leads, more customers, and more foot traffic. While this is an effective way to build a business, it is costly and time consuming. It requires constant and consistent effort, and while this approach does generate results, those results quickly disappear when the effort stops or becomes less intense.

Successful businesses that see sustained growth have a double-edged marketing strategy. They focus their efforts *outward* on new potential customers and marketing, as well as *inward*, on existing customers and referral business.

These successful businesses have leveraged their existing efforts to generate more revenue. Simply put, their customers buy from them time and time again.

For most businesses, this is the easiest way to increase their revenues. Simple customer loyalty strategies and outstanding customer service are often all you need to dramatically increase your sales from the customers you already have.

The Cost of Your Customers

Do you know how much it costs your business to buy new customers? Each new customer that walks through your door, with the exception of referrals, has cost you money to acquire. You have spent money on advertising and promotions to generate leads and turn those leads into customers.

For example, if you have placed an ad in your local newspaper for $1,000, and the ad brings in 10 customers, you have paid $100 to acquire each customer. You would need to ensure each of those customers spent at least $200 to cover your margin and break even.

Alternately, if you spent two hours of your time and $10 per month on an email marketing program to send a newsletter to your existing database of customers, and you bring in 10 customers as a result – each customer has cost you $1.

Generating more repeat business means focusing on the marketing strategies that aim to keep your existing customers instead of purchase new ones. This effectively reducing the cost of attracting new customers to your business.

These strategies are simple to implement, and do not require much time investment. Just a solid understanding of how to make customers want to come back and spend more of their money

Keeping Your Customers

Marketing strategies that focus on keeping your current customer base are easy and enjoyable to implement. They allow you to build real relationships with the people you do business with, instead of dealing with a revolving door of people on the other end of your sales process.

Repeat customers create a community of people around your business that presumably share the same needs, desires and frustrations. The information you gain from these customers (market research) can help you strengthen your understanding of your target audience, and more accurately segment it.

Remember   80% of your revenue comes from 20% of your customers. Always focus on these customers. They are ideal customers that you want to recruit and hold on to.

Customer Service: Make them love buying from you

Every business, even those with excellent service standards, can improve the service they provide their customers. Customer service seems to be a dying concept in most businesses; more focus seems to be placed on the speed of the transaction. These days you can even go to the grocery store now and not speak to a single sales associate thanks to self-serve checkouts.

To improve your company's customer service standards, take a survey of your customers and your employees to brainstorm ways you can improve the experience of buying from your business.

Successful customer service standards those that make your customers *buy* are:

Consistent. The standards are up kept by every person in your organization. Expectations are clear and followed through. Customers know what to expect and choose your business because of those expectations

Convenient. It is nearly effortless for the customer to spend money at your place of business. Convenience can take many forms; location, product selection, value-added services like delivery and it is also consistent.

Customer-driven. The service the customer receives is exactly how they would like to be treated when buying your product or service. It is reflective of your target market, and appropriate to their lifestyle. Customers would probably not appreciate white linen tablecloths at a fast food restaurant, but they would appreciate a 2-minutes or less guarantee.

Newsletters: Keep in touch with your customers

A regular newsletter is an easy, time-effective, and inexpensive marketing strategy to implement. Unfortunately, many small businesses think these are too time consuming and too expensive to adopt as part of their marketing strategy.

The most popular type of newsletter distribution is email. This will cost your business as little at $10 per month for an email marketing service subscription and can be customized to your unique branding.

Here is an easy five-step process to starting a company newsletter:

1. Pick your audience. New customers? Market segment? Existing customers?

2. Choose what you're going to say. Company news? Feature product? New offer?

3. Determine how you're going to say it. Articles? Bullet points? Pictures?

4. Decide how it's going to get to your audience. Email? Mail? In-store?

5. Track your results. How many people opened it? Read it? Took action?

Value Added Service: Give them happy surprises

Adding value to your business is an effective way of getting your customers back. Every person I know would choose a mattress store that offered free delivery over one that did not. It's that simple.

There are many ways to add value to your business, including:

o **Feature your expertise.** Use your knowledge to provide additional value to your customers. Offer a free consumer guide or report with every purchase.

o **Add convenience services.** Offer a service that makes their purchase easier, or more convenient. The best example of this is free shipping or delivery.

o **Package complementary services**. Packaging like items together creates an increase in perceived value. This is great for start-up kits.

o **Offer new products or services**. Feature top of the line or exclusive products, available only at your business. Offer a new service or profile a new staff member with niche expertise.

Value added services generate repeat customers in one of two ways:

1. Impress them on their first visit. Impress you customer with great service, a product that meets their needs, and then wow them with something extra that they weren't expecting. Get them to associate the experience of dealing with your business with happy surprises and create a perception of higher value.

2. Entice them to come back. The introduction of a new value-added service can be enough to convince a customer to buy from you again. Their initial purchase established a trust and knowledge of your business and its processes. They will want to "be included" in anything new you have to offer, especially if there is exclusivity. It is easier to attract clients that have purchased from you than potential clients who have not.

Customer Loyalty Programs: Give them incentives

Another simple way to keep in touch with existing customers and keep them coming back to you is to create a customer loyalty program.

These programs do not have to be complicated or costly and are relatively easy to maintain once they have been implemented. These programs help you gain more information on your customers and their purchasing habits.

Here are some examples of simple loyalty programs that you can implement:

Free product or service. Give them every 10th (or 6th) product or service free. Produce stamp cards with your logo and contact information on it.

Reward dollars. Give them a certain percentage of their purchase back in money that can only be spent in-store. Produce "funny money" with your logo and brand.

Rewards points. Give them a certain number of points for every dollar they spend. These points can be spent in-store, or on special items you bring in for points only.

Membership amenities. Give members access to VIP amenities that are not available to other customers. Produce member cards or give out member numbers.

Remember, for this strategy to work, you and your team must understand and promote it. The program becomes a product that you sell.

8

Profits from Fresh Air

As a small business owner, you are in business for one reason: to make money.

Of course, there are other reasons you started or purchased your company. You may love the product you sell, or service you provide. You may love the challenge of turning a floundering company into an overnight success. You may just love being your own boss. Naturally, this all means nothing if you are not generating enough income to support yourself and your family, as well as the people who work for you.

Nearly all businesses make money. Unless not a single product or service is sold, there is always money coming in. But there is also always money going out. Supplies, wages, marketing, acquisitions and operations all contribute to the expense of just staying in business.

Simply put, profit is the difference between money in and money out. This is the dollar value of your sales, minus the cost of those sales.

In business, you will find that everyone wants to make more money. They want to increase their sales, get more money coming in. **What often gets overlooked is that the true secret to making more money is not increasing sales but increasing profit.**

What is Profit?

Before you can take steps to increase the profitability of your business, you need to have a solid understanding of:

- Types of profit
- What factors influence profit
- What your profit is *right now*

Types of Profit

There are two main types of profit:

Gross Profit

Gross profit is the simplest form of calculating profit. It is simply the money that comes through the cash register, minus the cost of acquiring or providing the products or services. The formula is:

Total revenue (sales) – cost of goods or services sold = Gross Profit

Net Profit

Net profit is a more accurate reflection of your income. It is calculated by taking your gross profit minus expenses over a specific time period (usually by quarter). The formula is:

Gross profit – expenses (cost of running a business) = Net Profit

Factors that Influence Profit

Profit is your bottom line. It is the number that falls out the bottom when all other costs and expenses have been taken into consideration. Do you know what contributes to the amount of profit your business ends up with?

There are three main factors that influence profit:

Sales – Your Conversion Rate

The first, and most obvious, factor is the money that comes in the door through sales. In theory, the more sales you make, the more money you bring in, the greater your profits. The ratio of potential customers to sales is called your conversion rate. This is the percentage of customers you have converted from leads to sales. So, a high conversion rate means more sales, and more money coming in the door.

In addition to your conversion rate is the lifetime value of your clients. It costs much less to convince a customer to make repeat purchases than it does to acquire new clients.

Costs – Your Product/Service Margins

The second factor is the cost of your offering. What your product or service costs you to acquire or provide. If you sell a product, this is the wholesale price you pay for the product. If you offer a service, it is the cost of your (or your employee's) time plus any materials used.

Your margin is the difference between the price you pay and the price your customers pay. If you buy toothpaste for $1 from the wholesaler, and you sell it for $3, your margin is $2. If a haircut costs $20 in materials and service, and the customer pays $50, your margin is $30.

Expenses – The Cost of Doing Business

The final factor is the cost of running your business. These are costs not directly related to the specific product or service you offer. Expenses include:

- Office or store lease
- Computer equipment lease

- Employee salaries
- Utilities
- Marketing and advertising

Your Profit

It only makes sense that you need to know where you are to determine how to get to where you want to be. This applies to any plan to create in business.

Before you can increase your profits, you need to understand where your profits are currently. The next section will take you through a process to review the specific factors that affect your business's profitability, and ultimately determine how much profit you are currently bringing in.

Taking Stock of Your Profits

Before you devise a strategy to increase your profits, you need to take a good long look at the money your business brings in, and the money you spend to run your business. You may wish to sit down with your accountant or bookkeeper to analyze the financial information that is available to you. Decide on a specific time period to review. Choose one that makes sense to your business, and one that will give you the most realistic picture of your business performance.

This will depend if your operation is cyclical or remains steady throughout the year. Usually, the previous quarter or the previous four quarters will give you enough of an indication.

Review the following items:
- Total revenue
- Total cost of goods or services

- Total cost of operations (overhead), including:
- Employee wages
- Recruitment
- Business development
- Utilities
- Rent or mortgage
- Office supplies
- Computer leases
- Incidentals
- Total cost of marketing campaigns

Total profit after costs and expenses for this time period: _____.

The Five Factors that Eat Your Profits

It is easy for business owners to compare their organizations to the apparent success of their competitors. Joe's Pizza may always be overflowing with customers and appears to be making money hand over fist, while your pizza shop may have slower, but more steady business. Do not confuse bodies in a chair with bottom line profits.

It is important to remember that a business with extraordinary sales figures is not necessarily a profitable one. Sales are just one element of your profit calculation. Here are some other elements to think about when reviewing the profitability of your business:

Impulse Spending

How often do you make purchases for your business operations? I'm not talking about acquiring new goods and services, but upgrading computers, taking your team out for lunch, or leasing a new color photocopier.

Do you allow your staff to make purchases on your behalf? Who reviews these decisions? Look not only at *what* you buy, but *how* spending is structured in your company.

Small Margins

As we discussed in the previous section, your margins are the difference between your cost and the customer's cost to purchase your goods or services.

Typically, businesses that offer a variety of products will have both products with large margins, and products with small margins. The products with large margins generate the most income, so these are the products that staff should be focused on selling. What many businesses overlook is that products with small margins will never generate a high level of income, no matter how many you sell. A store stocked with small margin items will never be able to increase their profit because they have so little margin to work with.

Your Customers

This may seem like a backwards way of thinking. Your customers spend money, so they are a positive factor in your profit calculation, right?

This is true for most of your customers. But remember the 80/20 rule of business – 80% of your revenue comes from 20% of your customers. These are your top 20%, or ideal customers. What about your bottom 20%? The group of clients who ask for the moon and never stop complaining. These clients can be a huge drain on both your staff resources and your financial resources. Their true value to your business is minimal and they cost more than they bring in. Fire them!

Loan Interest

How many business loans do you currently have? Credit card debit? Overdraft? The interest you pay on these loans can be a substantial monthly cost to your business.

A loan from a bank is just like any other product. You can shop around for the best deal. Consider consolidating or restructuring your debit to minimize interest payments. Plan to search around for the best rate every few months or quarter.

Vendors

Do you purchase your goods and services from a wholesaler or retailer? How long have you been in business with this company? What do you pay for goods and services relative to your competitors?

Ensure that you are dealing with as direct a vendor as possible to minimize your acquisition costs and increase your margins. If you have been doing business with a specific vendor for an extended period of time, consider renegotiating your business arrangement.

The Basics of Increasing Profit

Your Profitability Goal

Now that you understand the current profitability of your company, it is time to look at ways to increase your bottom line. Like all other aspects of your business development, you need to have a clear idea of your intention or purpose before you begin any activity. Assuming you wish to increase the profitability of your business, you need to determine by how much and within what time frame.

Create a profit-related goal for your business, and write it here:

_____

_____

Three Ways to Increase Profit

There are countless strategies for increasing profit, but ultimately you can only increase profit in one of three ways:

1. Get More Customers

Use marketing outreach strategies to generate more leads and convert those leads into more customers. Introduce a new offer, expand your target audience, or approach a new target audience.

2. Get Your Customers to Buy More Often

Use customer loyalty and retention strategies to get your existing customers to buy from you more often. Make it easy for them to come back and do business with you.

You can do this by adding value to your product or service, keeping in touch on a regular basis, and giving your customers incentive to make repeat purchases. Customer service is also an overlooked component of building a repeat client base.

3. Increase How Much Your Customers Buy

You'll naturally increase your sales when you increase the number of customers and how often they purchase. The final way you can impact your profit is by increasing the average dollar value of each sale. This can be achieved by up-selling every customer, creating package offers, and finding ways to increase the perceived value of your offering to justify increasing the price.

Managing Costs

One important way to impact the profitability of your business is through cost or spending management. Controlling how much money goes out will help you ensure that a more money stays in your bank account.

Remember, however, that cutting costs can only help increase your profits so much. There is a point where you will no longer be able to reduce expenses, and you will have to focus on increasing sales.

Why Cut Costs?

Cost management may seem like an obvious way of maintaining a healthy business, but it is also one of the primary reasons 80% of small businesses fail. Overspending is a huge problem for most businesses, and they don't even realize it.

Reducing costs is a great short-term strategy to boost profits. As I mentioned above, there is a limited amount of impact cost management can have on the bottom line, so it is an ineffective long-term strategy.

Cost management can also help you to generate more capital. A business that closely monitors and controls its spending is a much more desirable loan candidate than a business that spends freely. Most importantly, this strategy will help keep your business profitable through high and low periods. It's easy to spend money when your company is doing well, but this leaves little in the "just in case" account for downturns in the economy or unexpected expenses.

Where Can I Cut Costs?

Financing

As I mentioned, interest rates are a big culprit when it comes to eating profits. Take stock of how much money you are spending on a monthly basis in loan and interest payments. Can this be reduced? Is there another bank that will offer you a lower rate? Is there a way to consolidate these loans into a single, low-interest account?

Alternatively, if your business is doing well and has a large amount of money sitting in the bank; consider investing it or placing it in a high-interest savings account. Let your money make you money instead of spending it on unnecessary business luxuries.

Suppliers or Vendors

Again, make sure the price you pay for goods and services, for resale or internal, use is the lowest you can find. Try to deal directly with the manufacturer or distributor and renegotiate discounts and contracts with your vendors every year.

Hours of Operation

Evaluate the hours you are open for business each day, and why you have chosen the specific timeframe. Is it to compete with the competitors? Is it because you can serve the highest number of customers? Each hour you are open for business costs money, so make sure you are operating under the most ideal timeframe.

Staffing, Wages, and Compensation

This can be a sensitive subject for any business owner or employee. It is important to look at staffing redundancies and capacity levels, as well as hiring needs, when evaluating cost management strategies.

Do you need to hire new staff, or can you build capacity within your existing employees? Is there another way to compensate staff, or provide performance incentives that are non-monetary, have a high perceived value, and inexpensive for your business? Remember to take time and care when implementing any changes in this area of cost management.

Place of Business

If you operate an office in a downtown metropolis, you are going to have substantially higher operating costs than a competitor who runs an office just outside the city limits.

Make sure you can justify your location, and the amount of money you spend to be there. Consider the following questions:

- Are my customers impacted by where I do business?
- Do my customers need to visit my office?
- What impression does my business need to present?
- Do I need parking facilities?
- Do I need to be visible?
- Do I have staff to employ?
- Am I near public transit, lunch outlets, and other amenities?
- Do I need access after business hours?
- Should I lease or buy?
- What other costs are specific to this location?

Eliminate the invisible!

What could you and your staff live without? What wouldn't you notice if it just disappeared one day? Take stock of expenses that are not being properly used or appreciated. Think of amenity-based items, or convenience costs, like:

- Gym Memberships
- Morning refreshments (muffins, donuts, etc.)
- Publication Subscriptions
- Designer coffee and tea
- Fancy collateral packaging

Your Pricing Strategy

The cost of your goods and services have a direct impact on the money you bring in. Your pricing strategy is so important to your business that can even determine your success.

Deciding how much to charge for your product or service is a challenging task. You need to factor in your own costs, the product or service's perceived value, and the going rate. Ultimately, you want to be able to charge as much as possible for each item, without overpricing yourself out business.

Avoid the Lowest Pricing Strategy

The days of the lowest price guarantee and pricing wars are over. Especially for small businesses. The "big players" in the marketplace will quickly put you out of business if you try to compete on price. Their pockets are deeper, and they have lower operating costs due to their sheer size. They can afford to, you can't. If your customers leave for a cheaper alternative, they are not loyal customers.

Clearly Position Your Company and Your Offering

How do you want your target market to view your business, and your products? Are you trying to create an image of high quality? High value? Reliable service? Make sure your pricing is consistent with the image you are trying to project. If you are operating a high-end spa, you're not competing with the budget nail salon down the street, so your prices should be considerably higher.

Have a Good Working Understanding of Your Margins

Know how much the product or service costs you to offer before you establish a price. Do these costs remain consistent, or do they fluctuate? Restaurants that offer high quality meat and seafood often price their meals at "market rates" as opposed to fixed rates. Calculate the fixed and variable costs associated with your product or service. You will want to work the cost of the product or service, a percentage of your overhead, and your own profit into the cost of each item.

Pay Attention to Factors Beyond Your Control

Be aware of any government or industry regulations on the price of your product or services. Some laws will limit how much you can charge for standard services. For medical and dental services, most insurance companies will put a cap on how much a customer will be compensated for each service. Seek out all external factors that could impact your pricing.

Price with a Purpose

Your pricing strategy should be purpose focused. What exactly are you trying to do by setting your prices at certain levels? Here are some potential reasons for pricing strategies:

- Short-term profit increase
- Long-term profit increase
- Customer generation
- Product positioning
- Revenue maximization
- Increase margins
- Market differentiation
- Survival

Pricing Strategies

Cost Plus Pricing

This is the most basic pricing strategy. Set your price at a number that includes:

- Cost of goods or services, based on a specific sales volume
- Percentage of expenses
- Profit margin (markup)

Target ROI Pricing

Set your price at a rate that will achieve a specific Return on Investment target. If you need to make $20,000 from 1,000 units, or $20 per unit, then set your price at $20 more than cost, plus expenses.

Value Based Pricing

This can be a bit of an arbitrary pricing strategy, but it can also be the most profitable. Set your price based on the value or added benefit it brings to a customer. For example, if your product only costs you $40 to produce, but will save the customer $2,000 per year in energy costs, a price of $150 or $200 would not appear to be unreasonable in the eyes of the customer.

Psychological Pricing

What messages are you trying to send the customer when they're looking at your prices for your products? Do you offer the best deal? The highest value? These are reasons to choose prices that are higher or lower than the competition.

Pricing Guidelines

Price higher than cost. This may seem obvious but ensure that your pricing not only covers your costs, but potential fluctuations in sales volume and in the marketplace. If you sell half of your order, will you still make a profit?

Include expenses. If you price to cover your costs, will you also be able to cover your expenses and still see a profit? Your margin needs to pay for your expenses, leave you with something to live on, plus some working capital for the company.

Consider the 'fair' price. What do your consumers think is 'fair' for each service or product? This is impacted by your competitor's price, your company's image (high quality or high value, low cost), and the perceived value of your product or service.

Strategies to Increase Profit

Once you have a concrete understanding of where your business stands today in terms of profitability, minimized your operating costs, and restructured your pricing strategy, you can focus on other strategies to increase profit.

There are countless strategies and tactics that will help you to bring in more customers, get those customers to come back, and get those customers to spend more when they do.

Here is a list of ideas, many of which are covered in detail in other sections of this program:

- Advertise
- Establish an online presence
- Sell more high margin items
- Generate more leads
- Focus on referral business
- Increase customer loyalty and repeat business
- Increase conversion rates
- Restructure your team
- Reinvent your product
- Sell your intellectual capital

9

Systemizing Your Business and Developing Effective Processes

One of the biggest mistakes a business owner can make is to create a company that is dependent on the owner's involvement for the success of its daily operations. This is called working "in" your business. You're writing basic sales letters, licking stamps, and guiding staff step-by-step through each task.

There are several problems with this approach. One is redundancy. You're paying your staff to carry out tasks that you eventually complete. The second is poor time management. You're spending your day, at your high hourly rate, on tasks as they arise, leaving little room for the tasks you need to be focused on.

However, the biggest issue I have with this approach is that countless intelligent business owners are spending most of their time operating their business, instead of *growing* it. A good test of this is to ask yourself, what would happen if you took off to a hot sunny destination for three weeks and left your cell phone, PDA and laptop at home. Would your business be able to continue operating?

If you said no, then this chapter is for you. Systemizing your business is about putting policies and procedures in place to make your business operations run smoother. And more importantly, without your

110

constant involvement. With your newfound free time, **you will be able to focus your efforts on the bigger picture: strategically growing your business.**

Why Systemize?

For most small business owners, systems simply mean freedom from the day-to-day functioning of their organization. The company runs smoothly, makes a profit, and provides a high level of service, regardless of the owner's involvement.

Systemizing your business is also a healthy way to plan for the future. You're not going to be working forever. What happens when you retire? How will you transition your business to new ownership or management? How will you take that vacation you've been dreaming of?

Businesses that function without their ownership are also highly valuable to investors. Systemizing your business can position it in a favorable light for purchase and merit a high price tag.

A system is any process, policy, or procedure that consistently achieves the same result, regardless of who is completing the task.

Any task that is performed in your business more than once can be systemized. Ideally, the tasks that are completed on a cyclical basis; daily, weekly, monthly, and quarterly should be systemized so much so that anyone can perform them.

Systems can take many forms. From manuals and instruction sheets, to signs, banners, and audio or video recordings. They don't have to be elaborate or extensive, just provide enough information in step-by-step form to guide the person performing the task.

Benefits of Business Systems

There are unlimited benefits available to you and your business through systemization. The more systems you can successfully implement, the more benefits you'll see.

- Better cost management
- Improved time management
- Clearer expectations of staff
- More effective staff training and orientation
- Increased productivity and profits
- Happier customers and consistent service
- Increased staff respect for your time
- Increased level of individual initiative
- Greater focus on long-term business growth

Taking Stock of Your Existing Systems

The first step in systemizing your business is taking a long look at the existing systems in your business. At this point, you can look for any systems that have simply emerged as "the way we do things here."

How do your staff answer the phone? What are the processes customers go through when dealing with your business? How are employees hired? Trained? How is performance reviewed and rewarded?

Some of your systems may be highly effective, and not require any changes. Others may be ineffective and require some reworking. If you have previously established some systems, now is a good time to check-in and evaluate how well they are functioning.

Use the following chart to record what systems currently exist in your business.

Existing Systems

Administration	
Financials	
Communication	
Customer Relations	
Employees	
Marketing	
Data	

Seven Areas to Systemize

There is no doubt that system creation, especially when none exist to begin with, is a daunting and time-consuming task. For many businesses, it can be difficult to determine where to start to make the best use of their time from the onset.

Here are seven main areas of your business you can to systemize. Begin with one area and move to the other areas as you are ready. Alternately, start with one or two systems within each area, and evaluate how those new systems affect your business. Each business will require its own unique set of systems.

1. Administration

This is an important area of your business to systemize because administrative roles tend to see a high turnover. A series of systems will reduce training time and keep you from explaining how the phones are to be answered each time a new receptionist joins your team.

Administrative Systems	
Opening and closing procedures	Filing and paper management
Phone greeting	Workflow
Mail processing	Document production
Sending couriers	Inventory management
Office maintenance (watering	Order processing
plants, emptying recycle bins, etc.)	Making orders

2. Financials

This is one area of systems that you will need to keep a close eye on, but that doesn't mean you have to do the work yourself. Financial management systems are everything from tracking credit card purchases to invoicing clients and following up on overdue accounts.

These systems will help to prevent employee theft and allow you to always have a clear picture of your numbers. It will allow you to control purchasing and ensure that each decision is signed-off on.

Financial Systems	
Purchasing	Profit / loss statements
Credit card purchase tracking	Invoicing
Accounts payable	Daily cash out
Accounts receivable	Petty cash
Bank deposits	Employee expenses
Cutting checks	Payroll
Tax payments	Commission payments

3. Communications

The area of communication is essential and time consuming for any business. Fax cover letters, sales letters, internal memos, reports, and newsletters are items that need to be created regularly by different people in your organization.

Most of the time, these communications aren't much different from one to the next, yet each are created from scratch by a different person. There is a huge opportunity for systemization in this area of your business. Systemized communication ensures consistency and company differentiation.

Communication Systems	
Internal memo template	Newsletter template
Fax cover template	Sales letter template(s)
Letterhead template	Meeting minutes template
Team meeting agenda	Report template

| Sending faxes | Internal meetings |
| Internal emails | Scheduling |

4. Customer Relations

Another important area for systemization is customer relations. This includes everything the customer sees or touches in your company, as well as any interaction they might have with you or your staff members.

Establishing a customer relations system will also ensure that new staff members understand how customers are handled in *your* business. It will allow you to maintain a high level of customer service, without constantly reminding staff of your policies. It will also ensure that the success of your customer relations and retention does not hinge on you or any other individual salesperson.

Customer Relations Systems	
Incoming phone call script	Sales process
Outgoing phone call script	Sales script
Customer service standards	Newsletter templates
Customer retention strategy	Ongoing customer communication
Customer communications	strategy
templates	Customer liaison policy

5. Employees

Create systems in your business for hiring, training, and developing your employees. This will establish clear expectations for the employee and streamline time consuming activities like recruitment.

Employees with clear expectations who work within clear structures are happier and more productive. They are motivated to achieve 'A' when they know they will receive 'B' if they do. Establishing a clear training manual will also save you and your staff the time and hassle of training each new staff member on the fly.

Employee Systems	
Employee recruitment Employee retention Incentive and rewards program Regular employee reviews Employee feedback structure	Staff uniforms or dress code Employee training Ongoing training and professional development Job descriptions and role profiles

6. Marketing

This is likely an area in which you spend a large part of your time. You focus on generating new leads and getting more people to call you or walk through your doors. These efforts can be systemized and delegated to other staff members.

Use the information in this program to create simple systems for your basic promotional efforts. Any one of your staff should be able to pick up a marketing manual and implement a successful direct mail campaign or place a purposeful advertisement.

Marketing Systems	
Referral program Customer retention program Regular promotions Marketing calendar Enquiries management	Regular advertisements Advertisement creation system Direct mail system Sales procedures Lead management

7. Data

While we like to think we operate a paperless office, often the opposite is true. Your business needs to have clear systems for managing paper and electronic information to ensure that information is protected, easily accessed, and only kept when necessary. Data management systems help you keep your office organized. Everyone knows where information is to be stored, and how it is to be handled, which prevents big stacks of paper with no place to go.

Ensure that within your data management systems you include a data backup system. That way, if anything happens to you server or computer software, your data, and potentially your business, is protected.

Data Management Systems	
IT Management	Client file system
Data backup	Project file system
Computer repairs	Point of sale system
Electronic information storage	Financial data management

Implementing New Systems

If you completed the exercise earlier in this chapter, you will have a good idea of the systems that are currently in place in your business. The next step is to determine what systems you need to create in your business.

To do this you will need to get a better understanding of the tasks that you and your employees complete on a daily and weekly basis. If you operate a timesheet program, this can be a good source of information. Alternately, ask staff to keep a daily log for a week of all the tasks they contribute to or complete. Doing so will not only give you valuable insight into their how they spend their time daily, but also involve them in the systemizing process.

Review all task logs or timesheet records at the end of the week, remove duplicates, and group like tasks together. From here you can categorize the tasks into business areas like the seven listed above or create your own categories.

Then, you will need to prioritize and plan your system creation and implementation efforts. Choose one from each category, or one category to focus on at a time. The amount you can take on will depend on your business needs, and the staff resources you have available to you for this process.

Remember that system creation is a long-term process. It is not something that will transform your business overnight. Be patient and focus on the items that hold the highest priority.

Creating Your Systems

There is a variety of ways you can create systems for your business, depending on the type of system you need and the type of business you operate. Some systems will be short and simple. It may seem silly, but a laminated sign in the kitchen that outlines step-by-step how to make the coffee, will save time. Others will be more complex – i.e., your sales scripts or letter templates.

One thing all your systems have in common is steps. There is a linear process involved from start to finish. Begin by writing out each of the steps involved in completing the task and provide as much detail as you can.

Then, review your step-by-step guide with the employee(s) who regularly complete the task and gather their feedback. Once you have incorporated their input, decide what format will you be using. Will it be a manual, laminated instruction sheet, sign, office memo, etc.

Testing Your Systems

Now that you have created a system, you will need to make sure that it works. More specifically, you need to make sure that it works without your involvement.

Implement the new system for an appropriate amount of time and then ask for input from staff, suppliers and vendors, and customers. Evaluate if it is informative enough for your staff, seamless enough for your suppliers, and if it meets or exceeds your customer's needs. Take that feedback and revise the system accordingly. You will rarely get the system right the first time, so be patient.

Systems will also need to be evaluated and revised on a regular basis to ensure your business processes are kept up to date. Structure an annual or bi-annual review of systems and stick to it.

Employee Buy-In

It will be nearly impossible for you to develop effective systems without the involvement and input of your employees. These are the people who will be using the systems, and who are completing the tasks on a regular basis without systems. They have a wealth of knowledge to assist you in this process. Employees can also draft the systems for you to review and finalize. This will make the systemization process a much faster and more efficient one.

It is also important to note that when you introduce new systems into your company, there may be a natural resistance to the change. People, including your employees, are habitual people who can become set in the way they are used to doing things.

Delegation

The final step to systemizing your business is delegation. What is the point of creating systems unless someone other than you can use them to perform tasks? This doesn't have to mean completely removing your involvement from the process, but it does mean giving your employees enough freedom to complete the task within the structure of the systems you have spent time and considerable thought creating.

After that, allow yourself the freedom of focusing on the tasks that you most enjoy, and most deserve your time. You will be able to create big picture strategies to grow your business and increase your profits.

10

Profits Through Building a TEAM
(Together Everyone Achieves More)

The people you employ, contribute directly or indirectly, on a daily basis to the strength and vitality of your business. You can't run your business alone, so you rely on their skills and support. In simpler words, your employees help you to make money.

But your employees are not just the people who arrive at your office every day and exchange effort for a paycheck. Their role is not just to build capacity and sell more or serve more.

Your employees are part of a potentially powerful group of people that you can leverage to put your business on the fast track to success. Your staff is more than the people who work for you. They are members of your team. They are the group of people who are collectively working to achieve the same objective or reach the same vision. I say they are more than just employees because their collective, cohesive value is much higher than their individual worth.

We all know that more people working on the same task will ensure the task is completed faster. In business, when you have more people working together on the same task, you save time, increase brainpower, and ultimately, **make more money**.

Corporate Culture

Corporate Culture has become a common buzzword when it comes to building a successful business, and rightly so.

Your corporate culture is the environment in which you run your business, and the environment in which your team members work. It is rooted in the vision, mission and beliefs of the organization, and dictates the "kind of office" and "kind of people" that work in that office.

Corporate culture is something that typically develops organically. The business owner and senior employees create a positive or negative environment based solely on who they are as people and how they behave as leaders. You simply can't avoid creating some type of corporate culture when you run a business.

You can, however, avoid creating a negative or unproductive corporate culture. Whether you are just starting out, or seeking to improve your workplace, you do have control over the type of environment in which you run your business.

Like most things in business, this won't happen overnight. However, with a clear idea of where you want to go, and what you want to create, you'll be well on your way to getting there.

Vision

Your company's vision statement should be a bold, clear, short sentence that every single one of your employees knows and understands. It is a roadmap to your idea of success; if you don't know what that looks like, how will you know when you achieve it?

If your goal is to create a highly profitable company, what does highly profitable mean? $1 million in annual sales? $3 million in annual profit?

Do you seek to become the industry leader in sprocket production? How will this be measured? How many sprockets will you have to produce to reach this goal?

The vision statement is a short summary of the long-term objective of the company. What the company will look like, produce, achieve; it is how you know the company is "successful."

Many companies either do not have a vision statement or they keep it a secret from their employees. It is only discussed in board meetings or management meetings. For a team to collectively work toward a goal, they need to know what the big picture objective is. They need to have buy-in in the company's direction and be communicated with on a regular basis.

Be proud of your vision. Keep it visible for staff. Post it on the wall, include it in internal communications, and connect day to day activities too it as often as possible.

Sample Vision Statements

Here are some real examples of corporate vision statements:

"At Microsoft, our mission and values are to help people and businesses through the world realize their potential." – Microsoft

"Give every customer a reason to believe...STAPLES Business Depot—That was easy!" – Staples Canada

"To build the largest and most complete Amateur Radio community site on the Internet." – eHam.net

Creating a Vision Statement

The process of creating a vision statement is something that you can work through alone, or in collaboration with your team. It is highly recommended to review the draft vision statement with your employees to ensure they understand and support the goals and objectives of the company.

Keep the following points in mind when crafting your vision statement:

- **Think big** – Why did you start or buy this business? What was your dream or purpose in doing so?
- **Think long-term** – Vision statements should last five to 10
- **Be specific** – Use numbers, dates, ratings systems and other ways of measuring success
- **Be succinct** – Use clear, short, simple sentences that are easy to repeat and remember

Mission

Your mission statement is a general description of how you are going to achieve your vision. This is a longer and more detailed statement that should include what your business is, who your customers are, and how you are different from (better than!) the competition.

Sample Mission Statements

"The Mission of McGill University is the advancement of learning through teaching, scholarship and service to society: by offering to outstanding undergraduate and graduate students the best education available; by carrying out scholarly activities judged to be excellent when measured against the highest international standards; and by providing service to society in those ways for which we are well-suited by virtue of our academic strengths." – McGill University, Montreal, Canada

"Starbucks purchases and roasts high-quality whole bean coffees

and sells them along with fresh, rich-brewed, Italian style espresso beverages, a variety of pastries and confections, and coffee-related accessories and equipment -- primarily through its company-operated retail stores. In addition to sales through our company-operated retail stores, Starbucks sells whole bean coffees through a specialty sales group and supermarkets. Additionally, Starbucks produces and sells bottled Frappuccino® coffee drink and a line of premium ice creams through its joint venture partnerships and offers a line of innovative premium teas produced by its wholly owned subsidiary, Tazo Tea Company. The Company's objective is to establish Starbucks as the most recognized and respected brand in the world." – Starbucks

Creating Your Mission Statement:

Here is a recommended process for completing your mission statement:

Step One: List your company's core strengths and weaknesses. What do you do well? What do you need to work on, or avoid doing?

Step Two: Who are your primary customers? Describe the types of customers you serve; both internal and external.

Step Three: What do your customers think of your strengths? What strengths are most important to them? Go ahead and ask them if you need to.

Step Four: Connect the strength that each customer values with its customer type. Write it in a sentence. Combine any redundancies.

Step Five: Organize your sentences in order of importance

Step Six: Combine your sentences into a paragraph or two. Elaborate on points as needed. This is your draft mission statement.

Step Seven: Consult with your staff and customers and ask for their feedback. Do employees support the statement? Can they act on it? Do customers want to do business with a company with this mission statement? Does it make sense?

Step Eight: Incorporate the feedback received and refine the statement until you are happy with it. Then publish it everywhere!

Culture or Values Statements

Your culture or values statement is the next step in the process. It describes how you and your staff will go about taking action (your mission statement) to achieve your objective (your vision statement).

Every family has their own belief system and way of doing things. Everything from cooking to cleaning to raising kids is determined by the family. Every company also has their own set of values when it comes to running a business. It reflects the unique personality of the organization.

Sample Culture Statement

Our Culture

* Values-based leadership. Our Credo outlines the values that provide the foundation of how we act as a corporation and as individual employees so that we continue to put the needs of the people we serve first.

* Diversity. It's our individual differences that make us stronger as a whole. We recognize the strength and value that comes when collaborative relationships are built between people of different ages, race, gender, religion, nationality, sexual orientation, physical ability, thinking style, personal backgrounds and all other attributes that make each person unique.

* Innovation. True innovation can only be fostered within a supportive environment that values calculated risk in order to achieve the maximum reward. At Johnson & Johnson Inc., we encourage and reward

innovative thinking, innovative solutions and an innovative approach in all that we do

* Passion. The deep desire to enrich people's lives – by delivering quality products and remarkable experiences that make their lives easier, healthier and more joyful.

* Collaboration. The unwavering belief that great results depend on the ability to create trusting relationships.

* Courage. The fearless pursuit of the unproven, unknown possibility – the willingness to take great risks for the benefit of the greater good.

- Johnson & Johnson Canada

Creating Your Culture Statement

Involve your team in creating your company's culture or values statement. Generally, this is a point-form document that reflects the beliefs of the company, its employees, and its customers.

It can be helpful to think about the type of people you currently employ, as well as the ones you may wish to employ. What are they like? What are their belief systems? What are their most important values?

Remember that the culture or values statement is usually the longest of the three statements – and that's okay.

Your Team Leaders

The strength of a team lies in the strength of the people who lead it. No group of people is effective without strong leadership, just like no business is effective without a strong owner or management team.

Building a strong team means knowing who your leaders are – both in job description and natural ability.

Understanding the strength of your natural leaders and the skills of your natural followers will allow you to strategically structure your team for maximum effectiveness and efficiency. It will give insight into who is best suited for management promotions and project management; which team members have the ability to assemble and motivate their peers.

Your leaders need to have a high degree of passion for your product or service, and truly believe in the company's vision. They need to be able to handle a high level of responsibility and manage a range of people to achieve a common goal. Your leaders are your team builders. They present new ideas, build consensus, and encourage the involvement of others.

Types of Leaders

Simply speaking, there are four main types, or styles, of leaders. I listed each description as well as which type of employee it works best for.

Autocratic:

- Classical or "old-school" approach. Manager holds all power and decision-making authority. No employee consultation or input. Orders are obeyed. Reward/punishment structure.
- New, untrained employees. Detailed orders and instructions are required. No other leadership style has been effective. Limited time available. Department restructuring. High production requirements.

Bureaucratic:

- "By the book" approach. All is done to specific procedures/policies. All tasks outside policies referred to higher management.
- Routine tasks performed. Standards and procedures need to be communicated regularly. Safety or training. Cash handling. Dangerous equipment

Laissez-faire:

- "Hands-off" approach. Employees have almost total freedom. Little direction or guidance is provided. Employees must make own decisions, set own goals. Employees must solve own problems.

- Highly skilled and experienced employees. Employees are highly driven and ambitious. Consultants are being managed. Employees are trustworthy.

Democratic:

- "Participatory approach". Employees part of decision -making process. Employees well informed. Leader has final say but involved others. Collaborative approach. Encourages employee development with guidance and assistance from leader. Leader recognizes and rewards achievement.
- Collaborative environment. Employee development and growth is the focus. Changes or problems affect employees and require their input to create a solution. Team building and participation is encouraged.

Communication

The only way to build and maintain a strong team is through strong, consistent communication. This is often an overlooked or neglected aspect of business management and is easily forgotten during periods of high stress or heavy workload.

Avoid letting communication fall on the backburner by creating a regular meeting schedule and sticking to it. Depending on the size and type of your business, daily, weekly, or monthly team meetings are an important cornerstone of a strong team.

Regularly scheduled team meetings are like Sunday dinners with a busy family. They give you, the owner, a regular forum with your staff to implement company-wide training initiatives, announce results, establish goals and targets, or share new visions or directions. They also give your staff a forum to share feedback and air grievances.

Effective Team Meetings

By now you're probably thinking, "Sure, I hear some company's team meetings are effective, but we tried them, and it didn't work," or "I held regular team meetings, but after a while, no one showed up."

There is a difference between team meetings held for the sake of having team meetings, and well-prepared team meetings with a purpose.

You need to start holding team meetings with a purpose.

Establish a Schedule That Everyone Can Commit To

Scheduling is potentially the biggest challenge when trying to set up a team meeting. Often, all your staff members are busy going in eight different directions to fulfill their roles and operating on dramatically different schedules.

This is one reason why regular team meetings are important. Ad hoc meetings require ad hoc scheduling and reduce the likelihood that all your team members will be able to attend.

Ask your team to block off one hour (or two) each week (or month) for the team meeting in a time slot that is convenient for everyone. Establish a clear attendance expectation from everyone. This will exclude that time slot from the scheduling of other meetings and avoid conflict.

If you find that a team meeting is not necessary one week, you can always cancel it.

Know Your Purpose

Each team meeting should have a purpose and clear objectives. Is it to educate? Build consensus? Gather feedback?

Once you have established a purpose for a particular meeting, send an agenda to your staff confirming the meeting and outlining your objectives.

This is a good time to ask if anyone has a subject they would like to raise at the meeting.

If you find you do not have a clear purpose or objective, ask yourself if a team meeting is the best use of time for that week and consider postponing it to the next regularly scheduled time slot.

Plan Each and Every Minute

The biggest complaint from employees about team meetings is the length. Too often team meetings run out of control and end up taking three hours instead of one. You will quickly lose team focus and respect for the regular meeting this way. By establishing a clear agenda and staying on topic, you can run an efficient, succinct meeting.

Your detailed agenda should include:

- meeting purpose or objective
- list of topics and associated speakers
- list of decisions that need to be made/agreed to
- time allocation for each topic
- opportunity for additional topics at the end

Circulate your agenda in advance of the meeting, and request input and feedback. When all team members have reviewed and contributed to the agenda, you will increase their level of ownership and buy-in into the process.

Establish the Facilitator

Choose one person to chair the meeting and keep it on track. This is generally the business owner or a senior member of the team with some authority over junior staff and a high level of respect.

It is the responsibility of the facilitator, or chairperson, to create an environment of open dialogue and trust, and to keep the meeting on schedule.

Create a Follow-up Schedule

Assign the task of taking detailed meeting minutes to a team member or rotate this responsibility on a regular basis. It is important to record what happens in team meetings, just as you would in a client-related business meeting.

In the minutes, establish a system for tracking the action items that arise from decisions made in the meeting. This can be set up as a simple chart:

Decision	Action	Responsibility	Deadline

Make sure that these responsibilities are assigned and agreed upon in the meeting, and clear deadlines are established. Reviewing or following up on this chart can serve as a regular topic during team meetings.

Circulate meeting minutes to all attendees and ask for input or revisions. You may wish to circulate meeting minutes with the agenda for the next team meeting and gather feedback at the same time.

Motivations + Incentives

A big challenge in team building is coming up with new ways to foster and maintain a high level of motivation. How do you keep teams of people excited and driven to succeed over long periods of time? How do you keep your team motivated to improve their performance, and increase their achievements?

It is important to note that we're not just talking about individuals, but teams of people working together. It is simple to motivate a single person, but an entire team of motivated people will generate significantly higher results.

The key here is to give incentives for individual and team accomplishments. Incentives that reward based on collective achievement require people to work together and motivate each other to succeed.

Before we start talking about monetary and incentive-based rewards, it's important to look at motivational factors that are not incentive-driven.

Room to Work

Employees who feel their managers and supervisors believe and trust in their abilities are happier and will always perform at a higher level than those who do not. They are motivated to "prove them right" and feel supported in their efforts.

Micromanagement quickly reduces morale. It is essential that you and your managers clearly express confidence in your team members. You hired them to do a job, perform a role, so you must ensure they have the space to do so.

When you put effective systems in place and establish clear expectations, you create a clear context or boundary system for employees to work within. They understand the decision-making hierarchy, and the general way 'things are done around here.'

Your team should be encouraged to take initiative and to take risks within this context. You have hired your team based on their skills and intellectual capabilities, and thus should be able to trust in their choices and decision-making abilities.

Incentives

Incentives are great motivators. An incentive is a reason to perform or act in a certain way. For example, if your team increases sales by 40% by month's end, they will be treated to an expensive dinner.

Incentives need to be specific and have deadlines in order to be effective. In the example above, sales need to increase by 40% by the end of the month for the team to receive their dinner. If sales only increase by 30%, or if they increase by 40% at the end of the second month, the team does not earn their reward.

Time-specific incentives increase the sense of urgency and encourage staff to work harder to achieve the objective. If the incentive is not time-bound, there is no reason to work faster or harder since staff will assume they will reach their milestone "eventually."

Rarity is also a key component of effective incentive-based team building. If the reward is ongoing (i.e., if staff receive an expensive dinner every month sales are over $75,000), then "there's always next time." There is a lesser incentive to push performance to receive the reward. Some team members may care one month, but not the next.

Monetary Incentives

Bonuses and salary increases are a popular way to give your team an incentive to perform. These can include:

- Commissions

- Bonuses for completing a challenging project, or hitting a target
- Rewards for highest producing employee
- Salary increases based on met targets

It's up to you how you choose to structure your monetary incentives, based on your budget and resources. Remember to ensure that the terms of each incentive are clearly outlined, and that both parties (you and your employee) understand the agreement.

Gift Rewards

Physical, tangible gifts are an inexpensive way to reward your team for achievements and improvement. These rewards show that you have given some level of thought to what they might enjoy or appreciate in exchange for a job well done. They're also a great way to surprise employees.

Here are some ideas:

- Spa gift certificates
- Books – *consider motivational or business-related topics*
- CDs or DVDs
- Meals – lunch or breakfast
- Other gift certificates – gas, food, meals, local shops
- Movie or theatre tickets
- Weekend getaway – hotel, meals, etc.
- Flowers
- Gym Memberships.

So What Do You Do From Here?

Take Action! Whether you're an accomplished business owner looking to enhance the speed of your business' success, or are just starting out and need guidance, the thing you must do is to act.

The best successes come from taking the time to work on yourself, studying successful businesses, and absorbing new marketing strategies. Once these small, but crucial practices become habits, success will naturally follow. The biggest setback people in business face, is not understanding the processes that pave the way for big successes. Successful business leaders take the time to learn the industry and gather the tools and knowledge it takes to run a thoughtful, efficient, and lucrative business.

If you have a business that is struggling to reach the outcomes you've hoped for, this how-to manual is a great place to start. The steps and processes outlined here will help you gather the right information, apply them to your individual situation, and will ultimately transform your business and your quality of life. If your business has not yet managed to start to create wealth that allows you to take time off, build retirement accounts or pay for your children's college, then learn and master the steps outlined in this book. Get the right information, find someone that knows how to walk you through them and watch your quality of life take new shape.

Be unique, own your industry and dominate your marketplace.

www.ingramcontent.com/pod-product-compliance
Lightning Source LLC
Chambersburg PA
CBHW060901170526
45158CB00001B/444

* 9 7 8 1 0 7 9 5 5 6 4 0 7 *